BOEING 747

BOEING 747

Robbie Shaw

OSPREY
AEROSPACE

First published in Great Britain in 1994
by Osprey, an imprint of Reed Consumer Books
Limited, Michelin House, 81 Fulham Road,
London SW3 6RB, and Auckland, Melbourne,
Singapore and Toronto

© 1994 Osprey Publishing

Reprinted 1996

ISBN 1 85532 420 2

Edited by Tony Holmes
Page design by Paul Kime
Produced by Mandarin Offset
Printed and bound in Hong Kong

Front cover This shot of Northwest Airlines 747-251B N615US shows the sheer bulk of its fuselage. Unlike any other airliner, the 747 can accommodate its passengers in the nose section, thus allowing them to benefit from much reduced noise levels

Back cover This worm's eye view clearly exposes the size of the huge trailing-edge flaps on the 747. The ability of Cathay Pacific pilots to land at Hong Kong in some of the worst weather conditions imaginable is legendary

Title page This head-on shot gives one an idea of the problems that confront pilots converting to the 747 from another type – for example, the height of the flight deck above the ground is far greater than any other airliner currently in service. It may take the pilot quite a few hours on-type to adjust to the landing and subsequent ground manoeuvring phases following his conversion onto the 'big Boeing'. The four main-wheel bogies, which are required to evenly distribute the weight of the jet when its on the ground are also visible from this ramp-level viewpoint. This particular 747 is a Series 100 airframe, and allocated the serial N611US, it wears the old Northwest Orient Airlines livery

Contents page With the advent of an aircraft the size of the 747, airports the world over had to physically adapt to the considerably larger dimensions of the new wide-bodies. Many could not expand apron space due to urban conurbations, and the vexing question of handling dozens of these aircraft daily took some solving. The answer engineers came up with was the airport 'jetty', where aircraft could simply nose up to the terminal and park – in turn, when it came time to leave, the 747 would be simply pushed back to the taxyway, rather than have to self-manoeuvre. To move a fully-laden 747 requires a powerful and very expensive tug, and those used by British Airways, for instance, have an engine capacity of 410 hp. Here, Tug 121 has just finished pushing back 747-200 G-BDXI *City of Cambridge* from Stand 54 at Gatwick's North Terminal. Note that the tug has a driver's cab at both ends, and that it can be raised by a few feet to improve his view when man-handling large aircraft

For a catalogue of all books published by Osprey Aerospace
please write to:

**The Marketing Department, Reed Consumer Books,
1st Floor, Michelin House, 81 Fulham Road, London SW3 6RB**

Introduction

If you were to ask anyone in the Western World, be they man, woman or child, to name a well-known aircraft, 90 per cent would come up with one of two answers; Concorde or the 'Jumbo Jet'. The latter is the nickname given to that mighty leviathan, the Boeing 747, which was the world's largest aircraft when launched back in 1969. 1994 saw the 25th anniversary of the type's first flight on 9 February 1969, and delivery to a customer – Pan American – on 12 December 1969. In a quarter of a century over 1000 'Jumbo Jets' have been delivered to the world's airlines. It is hoped this book will serve as a small tribute to an aircraft which has become one of the legendary designs in aviation history.

In the following pages the photo-captions will feature designations such as Boeing 747-136, so for those not familiar with company production numbers some explanation is necessary. Boeing assigns each customer a designation number, or number/letter. British Airways, for instance, is '36', therefore the Series 100s, -200s and -400s of British Airways are designated 747-136, -236 and -436 respectively, whilst Eva Air's designation is '5E', therefore its Series 400s are 747-45E.

Unless otherwise credited, all photographs in this volume were taken by me using Kodachrome 64 film. I would like to thank John Dern of the Boeing Airplane Company for his assistance.

Robbie Shaw
August 1994.

Contents

B747-100

The Boeing 747 is the world's largest, heaviest and most powerful airliner, yet its reason for being can be traced to the US Department of Defense who, in the early 1960s, issued a requirement for an ultra-large transport aircraft for the US Air Force. Boeing, along with rivals Douglas and Lockheed, submitted their proposals in the hope of winning a multi-billion dollar contract. In September 1965 the Secretary of Defense announced that the winning design was Lockheed's leviathan C-5 Galaxy. Although bitterly disappointed, all was not lost for the Boeing Company.

It was becoming apparent that despite the success of the 707, many of the airlines operating the type required an aircraft with even greater capacity. Unlike the DC-8, the design of the 707 did not favour a fuselage stretch, so in mid-1965 Boeing set up a small design team to work on a 'big brother' to the 707. When the announcement was made that Lockheed had won the USAF contract, the civil design team was joined by a similar group of Boeing engineers who had been working on the military project. This enlarged design 'think tank' was now set the task of producing a 'big' airliner as quickly as possible.

A number of concepts were discussed with prospective clients, including some rather innovative ideas such as side by side and upper/lower 'double bubble' fuselages. These were, however, firmly rejected early on in the project, and ultimately the design chosen was one based primarily on the 707, albeit on a much larger scale. This featured a lower, fuselage-mounted, swept-wing with four underslung engines and a sweptback tail fin. The influence of the military design team was evident with the flight deck re-located from the nose section to within a hump on the upper forward fuselage. This ensured that when a cargo variant of the 747 was proposed, no major redesign would be necessary for the basic airframe to successfully fill this demanding role, as it would allow wide loads access to the whole

Left 747-151 N601US is truly a veteran 'Jumbo'. The 27th built, it was the first of its type delivered to Northwest, who put it into service in April 1970. Like other 747s of the same age, this aircraft is still in regular use flying the US-Europe routes. Looking resplendent in its new livery, N601US is seen here just after take-off on yet another transatlantic flight in the summer of 1993

length of the fuselage, via loading through the nose, which could be swung open. In addition, the small space behind the flight deck could be converted into a passenger area, connected to the main cabin by means of a spiral staircase.

This latter feature particularly appealed to the airlines, the majority of whom have subsequently utilised it as a first-class lounge or a cocktail bar area. Another feature the airlines found attractive was the amount of underfloor space available for baggage and cargo, and many operators now accrue as much revenue from the cargo carried as they do from passenger fares. Thus, here on paper at least was a giant aircraft capable of carrying up to 500 passengers in a single class configuration, or about 350 in a mixed layout, over intercontinental routes. In addition, with the new turbofan engines that were then becoming available, the leviathan would be one the quietest and most fuel efficient airliners of its era, despite its size.

Boeing named this new model the 747, and its marketing teams set about the airline industry to persuade them to part with $20 million per aircraft. The commercial success of the 747 may, in part, be attributed to one man – Juan Trippe, President of Pan American. His airline first put the 707 into service, and this distinguished long-haul operator pulled off another coup a decade later when it stunned the aviation world on 13 April 1966 by announcing that it was to buy 25 747s. Boeing, however, still wanted more orders before committing itself to launching the jet, as only a small number of deposits had been received by Japan Air lines and Lufthansa.

In July the Boeing Company announced to the world that it was to proceed with the development and production of the 747, soon to be dubbed by the media the 'Jumbo Jet'. Plans called for the prototype to be completed by the end of 1968, with first airline delivery scheduled for September 1969.

This project was to be a huge one – several times the scale of the 707 programme. However, prior to the production of the 747 commencing there was the requirement for another mammoth task. The Boeing production facilities at Wichita, in Kansas, and at Renton, in the suburbs of Seattle, were already working to full capacity, and due to the compact size of the latter's airfield, it would not have been feasible in any case as site on which to build the new aircraft. Therefore, before the world's largest airliner could be built, the world's largest building, in terms of volume, had to be built from scratch.

The place selected was a 780-acre site at Everett, some 30 miles (45 kilometres) north of Seattle. Here, adjacent to the airport at Paine Field, a vast complex was built costing some $200 million. Work on the site began in the late summer of 1966, and by June of the following year construction of the first 747 at the complex had begun in earnest.

Above right About to rotate from Gatwick's runway 26L is Northwest's Boeing 747-151 N610US, seen here operating flight NW45 to Minneapolis/St Paul. This particular aircraft was delivered in November 1970, and is now surely in the twilight of its career as newer 'Jumbos' are delivered to the airline. Although Northwest has an ever-growing fleet of 747-400s, these are currently not flown to European destinations as their increased range makes them more suited to the airline's longer transpacific routes

Below right On a crisp December day in 1992 Northwest's 747-151 N603US climbs out of Gatwick en-route to Detroit as flight NW49. This aircraft looks as if it has just been accepted fresh from Everett Field, with not a wrinkle in sight, despite its 22 years of devoted service

Above In the 1980s Pan American World Airways decided to introduce a new livery, which dispensed with the traditional blue cheatline in favour of an all-white fuselage, with a natural metal belly. In place of the conservative titling, large, bold 'Pan Am' letters adorned the fuselage. Pan Am was synonymous with the 747, and it was a sad day in aviation history when this great pioneering airline ceased operations due to financial difficulties. Its first 747 service was to Heathrow, which is where 747-121 N749PA *Clipper Dashing Wave* was photographed in March 1989. This aircraft was delivered to the airline on 10 April 1970 and was originally named *Clipper Intrepid*

Left The nosewheel is turned almost 90° as this Pan Am 'Jumbo' enters runway 27L at London/Heathrow. This aircraft, N750PA, was delivered to the airline on 2 April 1970 as *Clipper Rambler* and began flying the airline's transatlantic routes three weeks later . It was photographed on 25 April 1990, just one day short of the aircraft's 20th year of service, by which time it had been renamed *Clipper Neptune's Favorite*. The aircraft was retired from service in 1991, and after a period in store at Marana Aircraft Park in Arizona, was broken up for spares

BIRTH OF A LEVIATHAN

Amazingly, whilst Boeing workers commenced construction of the first 747, much of the new plant was still being built around them. Everett was not, however, solely responsible for the assembly of the 'Jumbo', other divisions of Boeing throughout the US playing their part in the building of a legend. The factory at Wichita produced several components for the nose section, whilst a new plant at Auburn, some 20 miles (32 km) south of Seattle, was responsible for manufacturing wing panels. The same factory also built the main wing assembly jig for use at Everett.

Despite the size of the Boeing Company, the 747 would not have flown without the assistance of other major US aircraft manufacturers, as well as numerous aerospace component companies in almost every state, who were sub-contracted to produce parts ranging from rivets to main fuselage sections. The 'big' corporations involved included Fairchild, LTV, Northrop, and Rockwell, the latter building the lower centre fuselage section and wing leading-edges at its Tulsa, Oklahoma plant. In California Northrop produced components for the main fuselage, whilst Fairchild was responsible for the manufacture of all leading- and trailing-edge wing flaps, ailerons and spoilers. LTV's share of the work included the rear fuselage, tailplanes, vertical fin and the rudder – these items combined were considerably larger than the A-7 Corsair II, the last aircraft built by the Dallas company! Added to this of course were items from specialised manufacturers such as landing gear, engines and hydraulic systems.

In all, some four-and-a-half million items are required to build one 747, a process which takes about 21 months. Most of the component installation and sub-assembly work is completed by the time the aircraft begins to takes shape on the main production line, and only the final two months of this process are undertaken at Everett in the aircraft assembly hall

When the aircraft is almost structurally complete it is still unpainted, except for the rudder which is fully painted in customer livery prior to being fitted – this is because it has to be balanced before being attached to the tail assembly. At this stage the aircraft can now be moved on its own wheels to the fitting out bay, where electric, hydraulic, air-conditioning and pressurisation systems are connected. Here, also, myriad items ranging from toilets and galleys to the many signs which appear inside a modern airliner are installed. Seats and carpeting are also fitted at this stage, although some airlines prefer to fit their own after the jet has been delivered.

As the engines are fitted the cockpit instrumentation and navigation aids are added, and internally the machine is nearing completion. It is now time for the 'roll-out', and as the hangar doors are opened wide, the bare-metal structure slowly emerges under-tow by a powerful tug. Although unpainted, the metal appears dull and lifeless – this is due to a protective

Above right Tower Air is a New York-based 747 operator that flies passenger and freight charter services, as well as US military charters. The airline commenced operations in late 1983 with a single second-hand 747, but has since expanded considerably, and currently operates a fleet of 12 Series 100 and 200 747s. Illustrated wearing a simple all-white scheme, with bold fuselage and tail titles, is 747-127 N601BN. This former Braniff machine was Tower Air's first acquisition in November 1983, and was photographed about to rotate from the runway at the USAF base of Osan, in the Republic of Korea

Below right Following close on the heels of Pan American in introducing 747 services was rival operator TWA. Over the years this airline has reduced its fleet and network due to financial problems, and is now but a shadow of the company it once was. For instance, it now operates only 11 747s, a fleet which includes some of the oldest 'Jumbos' still flying anywhere in the world. Photographed at Heathrow in January 1994 is 747-136 N17125, a former British Airways aircraft (G-AWNI) that was acquired in March 1981, at which time it was almost 10 years old. Only weeks after this photograph was taken the 747 was sold to Tower Air, who currently operate it under the registration N605FF

Above Nationair was a Canadian airline which commenced charter operations in 1984 using McDonnell-Douglas DC-8s. During the summer season the bulk of its flights were transatlantic, whilst the winter saw Canadians fleeing to the warmer climes of Florida, the Caribbean and Mexico. A scheduled service was also launched linking Brussels and Montreal, and in 1992 a limited number of domestic schedules within Canada were also introduced. Soon after commencing its internal routes Nationair was hit hard by the recession, and the company ceased operations due to financial problems late in 1992 – its fleet had expanded to include six Boeing 757s and eight 747s by this point. The aircraft illustrated here taxying at Gatwick is a leased Series 101, registered C-FDJC. It was formerly Braniff Series 127 N602BN, which was later operated by Wardair as CF-FUN

Above right Photographed ready for take-off from runway 08R at Gatwick is Continental Airlines Boeing 747-143 N17011. This particular aircraft, the 78th 'Jumbo' built, has served with a number of operators over the years. It was delivered to Alitalia in March 1971 as I-DEME, but bought back by Boeing Equipment Holding Corporation ten years later. A succession of leases has seen the aircraft flying in the colours of Aer Lingus, Air Algerie, Icelandair, Overseas National, Pakistan International, SAS and Scanair. Finally, it was operating with People Express Airlines as N606PE when that company was bought out by Continental in 1987

Right Air Canada were quick to realise the potential of the 'Jumbo', and the airline ushered the new wide-body into service in April 1971, initially on the trans-Canada, Vancouver–Toronto, route. Within months the type was replacing DC-8s on transatlantic services to London, Paris and Frankfurt. The airline received five Series 133s, three of which are still in use alongside the same number of -233 Combis and -433 Combis. The aircraft featured here, 133 C-FTOC, was in its 21st year of service with Air Canada when photographed on its take-off roll on runway 23 at Glasgow's Abbotsinch airport in August 1992

Above Aer Lingus was the sixth European airline to receive 'Jumbos', the first of which arrived on 15 December 1970. Two Series 148 aircraft were initially acquired, and these were supplemented in 1979 by a former Lufthansa machine. These aircraft are used on routes from Dublin and Shannon to Boston and New York, and during the summer all three aircraft can be seen on the ground at Shannon in the space of a few hours. They are now most definitely in the twilight of their respective careers, and as this volume goes to press, the airline has just announced that the 'Jumbos' will be replaced in the summer of 1994 by Airbus A330s. Photographed on the taxyway at Shannon is EI-ASI *St Patrick/Padraig*. The name is written in English on the port side and Gaelic on the starboard

Left A close up view of a Pratt & Whitney JT9D-7 engine on Aer Lingus 747-130 EI-BED *St Kieran/Ciaran*. This aircraft formerly served with Lufthansa as D-ABYC *Bayern*, and is in fact even older than the Irish carrier's other two veteran 'Jumbos'

coating applied to prevent corrosion, which will not be removed until the aircraft is in the paint shop and ready to receive its customer livery.

The 'Jumbo' is now towed across a specially constructed 60-ft (18 m) wide bridge over a road to another part of the site which contains the paint shop and flight test areas, the latter being on Paine Field. A handful of systems tests are then completed, before the aircraft enters the 'paint shop', which is fitted with specially-controlled heaters to provide the optimum drying conditions. A typical 747 will receive on average some 250 gallons (565 l) of paint, and much masking off of the fuselage is undertaken whilst the airframe is in the paint shop – in fact, Boeing painters spend more time on preparing the 747 for spraying than they actually do decorating it!

The gleaming new aircraft will then be towed to the pre-delivery and flight test ramp, where it will be parked alongside up to ten other aircraft undertaking varying stages of final preparation that include filling the fuel tanks and looking for leaks, and systems checks prior to engine runs. The aircraft will also undergo two precise measuring operations; 1) a compass-swing to finely calibrate the aircraft's navigation equipment; and 2) the accurate weighing of the airframe. The latter is of vital importance because although each aircraft is constructed and assembled to the same exacting specifications, no two airframes will ever weigh the same.

Once the engine runs and other systems checks have been satisfactorily completed, the aircraft will move under its own power for the first time to undertake taxy tests. Then it is time for its maiden and initial test flights. These are flown by both Boeing and customer pilots, and following their successful conclusion the aircraft will be handed over to its proud new owner.

NUMBER ONE

The prototype 747, registration N7470, was rolled out on 1 September 1968 accompanied by great pomp and ceremony – and quite rightly so, as this great achievement had been completed a day ahead of the date planned at the start of the programme. The prototype was actually painted prior to the official roll-out ceremony, where it appeared in a red and white colour scheme, adorned with the logos of the 27 airlines who had ordered the type. After a series of high-speed taxy tests had been completed, the aircraft was fitted with additional instrumentation. This unfortunately took longer than originally planned, and the aircraft missed its scheduled maiden flight date of 17 December – a date specifically chosen to commemorate the 65th anniversary of the Wright Brothers first flight.

It was on 9 February 1969 that the 747 finally took to the air for the first time, with Jack Waddell, Boeing's senior experimental test pilot, at the controls, supported by two other flight engineers. After just one hour, however, the flight had to be cut short due to a minor malfunction with the

Above right Despite its age, 747-136 G-AWNE is still in use with British Airways. This aircraft was delivered to BOAC in March 1971, with whom it carried the name *City of Southampton*. The aircraft has since been renamed *Derwent Water* and, although Heathrow-based, was photographed at Gatwick on 31 October 1992 wearing 'Dreamflight' titles. These were applied for a 'one-off' flight carrying handicapped children to a holiday in Disneyland, the money having been raised by British Airways staff. Note 747s of Continental, Garuda and Virgin in the background

Below right Sporting a most innovative tail livery is Corsair 747-121 F-GIMJ. This airline performs charter flights from its Paris/Orly base with a fleet of two 737s and three 747s. The aircraft featured in this shot was the 47th 747 off the Everett production line, being delivered to Pan American as N754PA *Clipper Ocean Rover* on 26 May 1970. After a short period in storage in 1987, it was operated by Cargolux, Air France and Lionair under short leases, before joining Corsair in June 1990

trailing-edge flaps, and the aircraft returned to Paine Field.

A few more flights soon had things sorted well enough for the aircraft to land at Boeing Field, Seattle, where the remainder of the tests were completed. The next four aircraft built also joined the evaluation programme, with aircraft number two, the first for Pan American, appropriately registered N747PA and christened *Clipper America*. Its first flight was performed on 11 April 1969. Numbers three and four (N732PA and N731PA respectively) were also destined for Pan American, and the latter attended the 1969 Paris Salon at Le Bourget after a 5160-mile (8304 km) non-stop flight from Seattle.

At the show it was displayed alongside the prototype Concorde, the world's fastest airliner contrasting markedly with the world's biggest – these were heady days for civil aviation. The fifth and final aircraft to join the test fleet was N93101, the first 747-131 for Trans World Airlines (TWA). These five aircraft logged over 1400 flying hours between them during the ten-month long programme, which eventually culminated in the 747 receiving its FAA certification on 30 December 1969. The Pan American and TWA aircraft were then returned to Everett for refurbishing prior to delivery to their customer airlines. A further two airframes were also involved in the test programme, although neither actually flew as part of the evaluation process – one was used for detailed structural evaluation and the other for fatigue tests, both vital to the certification process.

Initial variants of the 100 Series were powered by Pratt & Whitney JT9D-1 engines. However, an unexpected increase in weight during construction of the 747 meant that the prototype's planned maximum take-off weight of 308,448 kg (680,000 lb) was increased to 322,056 kg (710,000 lb). The JT9D-1 engines struggled with this weight increase, and even their successor, the JT9D-3, was not an altogether satisfactory solution to this problem. It wasn't until the JT9D-3A was fitted that the aircraft performed to expectation, and the introduction of the JT9D-3AW, with water-injection, improved matters even further. Later production variants could also be fitted with General Electric CF6 or Rolls-Royce RB211 engines.

Although the Series 100 can seat up to 516 passengers, in the early years of service the configuration on most aircraft was such that the average capacity was in the region of 350 to 400 passengers, and today the range is typically somewhere between 370 to 450. The conservative seat allocation first introduced with the 100 Series reflected the economic reality of the early 1970s when transatlantic flying was still a luxury that few could afford. In those days only the affluent, and businessmen whose companies were picking up the tab, were regular passengers 'across the pond'. Transatlantic flight was still something that was almost unattainable to the average person in the street – that all changed later in the decade when personalities such as Sir Freddie Laker and his *Skytrain* brought

Above right With the 'Dunlops dangling', a Japan Air Lines 747 comes over the fence for a landing at Osaka International airport. Note that two of the mainwheel bogies are mounted in the belly and two in the wing, although all four retract into a cavernous bay in the belly itself

Below right Tokyo's Narita International sees more 747 operations per day than any other airport in the world, with around 75 per cent of flights into the airport being flown by Boeing's leviathan. Naturally, Japan Air Lines (JAL) account for a significant proportion of these, although US operators such as Northwest and United also operate into the airport in large numbers, much to the chagrin of JAL, who, with some justification, complain about the imbalance in the bilateral agreement between the two countries which blatantly favours the American carriers. This view, taken on a rather wet evening at Narita in 1986, features JAL examples from Series -100, -200 and -300, thus emphasising the sheer size of their fleet

transatlantic travel within the financial reach of millions of people.

Until then, however, the airlines could afford to have fewer seats in a more spacious cabin, and charge ridiculously high fares for those who could afford the privilege. For instance in economy-class areas the seating would be nine abreast in a three/four/two configuration, which compares to the three/four/three, ten abreast arrangement which is the norm today. As mentioned previously, many airlines also found the upper deck an attractive proposition, some using it exclusively for seating first-class passengers, whilst others converted the space into a cocktail bar and lounge, thus bringing back a small touch of the service once offered on the great transatlantic ocean liners of decades gone by.

One of the 'Jumbo's' greatest assets, however, is its cavernous hold, and I know of at least two airlines who have admitted, albeit unofficially, that they can still make a profit on a transatlantic flight even if there are no passengers, provided the hold is full of freight ! The amount of room on offer below the passenger deck is such that it can negate the need for a pure freighter in an airline's fleet, and many operators, including British Airways, don't have any dedicated 747F cargo haulers for this very reason.

When Pan American announced that it was to buy 25 747s at $21 million a copy, the gasps of shock reverberated around many an airlines' head office. Pan Am intended to launch its 747 service in December 1969, but due to those niggling engine problems, this had to be postponed until January 1970 – on the 22nd the inaugural 747 service was launched. This was on the prestigious 'Blue Ribbon' New York to London route, although this first flight was, in fact, delayed for several hours due to engine malfunction, and a substitute aircraft had to be made available. Luckily by this stage seven 747-100s had been delivered to the airline.

In the months that followed a number of destinations were added to Pan Am's 'Jumbo' network including Amsterdam, Barcelona, Brussels, Frankfurt, Lisbon, Paris and Rome, which were all served from New York. London's Heathrow airport soon became a second home for 747s in Pan Am's famous blue and white livery, as additional services connected it with Boston, Chicago, Los Angeles, San Francisco and Washington. When they had sufficient jets delivered, its 747s 'spread their wings' across the Pacific from Los Angeles and San Francisco to Honolulu, Hong Kong and Tokyo.

Whilst Pan Am's 747 network built up rapidly in a blitz of publicity, the second operator, TWA, began much more cautiously with a New York to Los Angeles service; New York–London followed in March 1970. Later that year the European capitals of Paris and Rome were added to the network, and its 707 fleet, like Pan Am's, either redeployed to thinner routes or were sold off. American Airlines also inaugurated a New York–Los Angeles service in March 1970, although this was performed with two aircraft leased from Pan Am, as American's jets weren't due for delivery until later

Above right Wearing All Nippon Airways' old colour scheme, 747-SR-81 JA8152 taxies to its parking spot at Naha airport, on the tropical island paradise of Okinawa. This photograph was taken in September 1986 when the airline was in the process of applying their new livery, many of their aircraft being grounded for overhaul at the same time

Below right Poised for a perfect landing at Osaka in April 1990 is All Nippon 747SR-81 JA8156. This aircraft features the airline's radically new livery, and as this particular jet solely operates on domestic routes, the fuselage titling is in Japanese characters only. All Nippon operate their SR variants in a 20/508 business/economy configuration, and as the average sector length is around one hour long, these aircraft accumulate an incredible amount of landing cycles compared to those on the long-haul routes

that year. March 1970 proved to be the peak for 747 production, with an amazing seven aircraft being produced that month.

The first foreign airline to commence 747 services was Lufthansa, whose first aircraft, D-ABYA (the 12th 747 built), first flew on 18 February 1970 and was delivered on 10 March. In April it replaced 707s on the Frankfurt–New York run. In the following months Air France and Alitalia also started services from their respective capital cities to New York. By the end of 1970 a further seven airlines, including Japan Air Lines and Iberia, had taken delivery of their 747s and put them into service – the remaining five operators were all US carriers; Continental, Northwest Orient, United, National and Delta, in that order. Northwest's network expanded quickly, and within months encompassed New York, Chicago, Seattle, Tokyo, Minneapolis/St Paul, San Francisco, Honolulu, Tokyo, Taipei and Hong Kong, whilst National and Delta at that time were purely domestic carriers.

In January 1971 two other American carriers, Eastern (again using leased Pan Am aircraft) and Braniff, also commenced 747 services. This was also the year that European carriers really got in on the act, with Aer Lingus, BOAC (now British Airways) and Sabena taking delivery of the first of their aircraft. However, due to an industrial dispute between pilots and the airline's management, BOAC's aircraft sat on the ground for almost a year before they were put into service. In the decades that have followed, the majority of the world's national carriers included 747s in their inventory.

One variant soon developed specifically for Japan Air Lines was the Boeing 747-100SR, the 'SR' standing for 'Short Range'. It was designed for high density, short-range, sectors, with a typical flight duration of one hour or less. The cabin configuration of these aircraft is ten abreast in an all-economy class and, due to the Japanese being somewhat smaller in physical stature than their western counterparts, the seat pitch is reduced to 33 inches, giving an all up capacity of no less than 516. Although externally identical to other Series 100 aircraft, the SR variant saw the strengthening of various items including the landing gear due to the extraordinarily high number of landings carried out during the type's life cycle. The first SR, the 221st 747 built, was rolled out on 3 August 1973 and flew for the first time on the last day of that same month. The SR is also used by Japan Air Lines' main competitor, All Nippon Airways.

The 747-100 series has enjoyed an extremely good safety record over its 25 years of service, and although the first loss occurred on 6 September

Right The camera catches the moment the port mainwheel tyres of this All Nippon 747SR-81 make contact with Osaka's runway after a one-hour flight from Tokyo's Haneda airport. There are some 20 ANA and JAL flights a day to Osaka from Narita and Haneda, most of which are operated by 747s

1970, neither Boeing nor the operator, Pan American, could be held responsible. The aircraft concerned, 747-121 N752PA *Clipper Young America*, was barely five months old when on a flight from Amsterdam to New York it was hijacked by Palestinian terrorists and flown to Cairo where, following the release of the passengers and crew, it was blown up. A Japan Air Lines aircraft also suffered a similar fate at Benghazi in 1973.

The first serious accident to occur befell Lufthansa's 747 D-ABYB *Hessen*, a Series 130, which crashed on take-off from Nairobi on 20 November 1974, killing 55 passengers and 4 crew. Fortunately, 85 passengers and 13 crew survived this accident. On 12 June 1975 an Air France jet was burnt out on the ground at Bombay when, after taxying to the ramp following a routine landing, the undercarriage caught fire, probably due to overheated brakes – fortunately there were no casualties. Over the years the 747 has entered the record books for setting new distance records for a single type, and for the number of passengers carried. However, the latter distinction was also the reason for an entry on 12 August 1985 that no one would have wanted; that of the largest number of casualties in a single aircraft accident.

Japan Air Lines 747-100SR JA8119 crashed on a domestic flight from Tokyo to Osaka after a sudden decompression had ruptured a bulkhead, which in turn seriously damaged all the flying controls and resulted in the crash. Only four of the 524 on board survived. Another Series 100 loss that will never be forgotten was that of Pan American's N739PA *Clipper Maid of the Seas* on 21 December 1988. Whilst en-route from Heathrow to Washington the aircraft was ripped apart by a terrorist's bomb, killing all 259 passengers and crew on board, and although the wreckage was spread over a wide area, major parts fell onto the small Scottish town of Lockerbie, where a further 11 died.

The main production of the 747-100 series was terminated early in 1976, although a few for Saudia and a number of SR variants were produced during the early 1980s. Including the prototype, a total of 207 Series 100 aircraft have been built, and despite many being now being over 20 years old, the majority are still in use today.

Right The sole 747-100 operated by Virgin Atlantic is G-VMIA. This aircraft began its operational career in 1970 as 747-123 N9669 of American Airlines, and after periods of lease to Cargolux, Highland Express, Qantas, Air Pacific and Aer Lingus, it was acquired by Virgin in 1990. Originally christened *Maiden Miami* by its new owners, in July 1992 it was renamed *Spirit of Sir Freddie* in honour of Sir Freddie Laker, who gave support to Richard Branson in his quest to sue British Airways over their 'dirty tricks' campaign. When Virgin ordered Airbus A340s it took the opportunity to revise its livery, dispensing with the red cheatline in favour of an all-white fuselage, and painting the engine cowlings red. G-VMIA was the first 747 to adopt the scheme, and it arrived at Gatwick on 18 February 1994 after painting

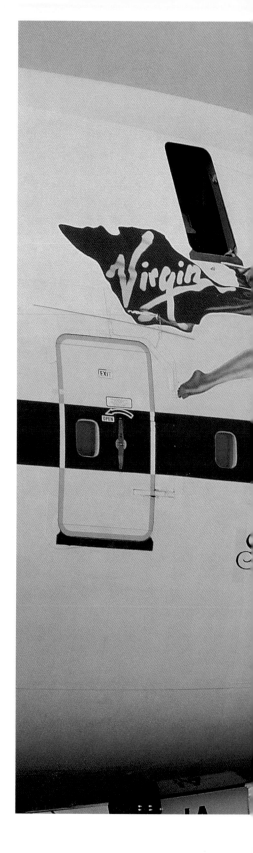

747-200 SERIES

Boeing quickly realised that their newest creation was capable of further improvement, particularly with the availability of better engines from the three major powerplant manufacturers. Added to this, Boeing went about strengthening the airframe and landing gear of the aircraft, thus enabling them to significantly increase the 747's maximum take-off weight, as well as allowing the customer the choice of an increase in payload or fuel – the latter obviously being the key to extending the aircraft's range. This version became known as the Boeing 747-200B.

The aircraft's external dimensions are the same as the Series 100, but a re-arrangment of the internal length of the upper cabin to the tune of an additional six feet slightly increased passenger capacity. To cater for this, an additional seven windows were installed in the top deck, bringing the total to ten. This minor change provides the only visible means of distinguishing a Series 200 aircraft from an earlier machine. The first Series 200 was in fact the 88th 747 built. It was rolled out on 27 August 1970, and during a test flight on 12 November set a world record for a commercial aircraft when it took off at a gross weight of 372,270 kg (820,700 lb). Registered as N611US, it was delivered to Northwest Orient soon after this flight, and is still in service with them today.

The second Series 200 was the first 'Jumbo' for the Dutch carrier KLM who, in February 1971, became the first airline to put this variant into service. Before the end of 1970 Swissair, Scandinavian Airlines System and Japan Air Lines had also taken delivery of their first -200s, with Alitalia, Air India, Condor, Lufthansa, Qantas, South African and Iberia following suit in 1971. The -200B soon proved to be the preferred model of the airlines, especially as more powerful engines became available, and the world record set by the first -200B was frequently bettered.

Right In addition to its fleet of elderly Pratt & Whitney powered Series 100 aircraft, British Airways also has a sizeable fleet of series -200 and -400 jets – both variants are powered by Rolls-Royce RB 211 engines. With the exception of seven Gatwick-based -200s, all of the airline's 'Jumbo' fleet are usually to be found at Heathrow. One of the 'magnificent seven', 747-236B G-BDXI *City of Cambridge*, is seen here departing its Sussex base on a flight to Lagos

The Series 200 airframe was also chosen by the US Air Force as an Airborne Command Post. Four were delivered to Strategic Air Command at Offutt Air Force Base, Nebraska, and given the USAF designations E-4A and E-4B. The latter featured more advanced communications equipment, and all have now been retrofitted to this standard. Much later, a further two were delivered to Andrews Air Force Base, Washington DC, for use as Presidential transports under the designation VC-25A. The pre-revolutionary Imperial Iranian Air Force (IIAF) also bought 747s, acquiring three ex-airline Series 100s and five new build -200s, although the last of these was never delivered – it was eventually acquired by Northwest.

Some of these aircraft were also adapted to carry Beech refuelling pods under the wings for the in-flight refuelling of fighter aircraft. IIAF 747s made regular visits to US air bases to pick up military supplies, but after the coup which ousted the Shah in 1979, relations with the America chilled, and the 747s were eventually disposed of, with the -200s going to Iran Air.

The freighter variant produced was the -200F, which featured an upward opening nose section – see the dedicated freighter chapter later in this volume for full details. Also utilising this feature was the -200C, which was a convertible passenger/freighter 747 with a strengthened floor. Unlike the purpose-built Combi variants of the 'Jumbo', the time taken to complete a role change in the -200C is considerable, and operators of this model tend to change the aircraft fit for a complete season to cope with maximum passenger and cargo demand, which tends to occur at different times of the year. The first -200C was built for World Airways and first flew on 23 March 1973. Another variant was the -200C(SCD), the acronym standing for 'Side Cargo Door', which is located aft of the wing on the port side of the fuselage and opens upwards. The launch customer for this variant was Iraqi Airways, whose first aircraft was delivered in June 1976.

One of the most popular variants of the 'Jumbo' is the 747-200 Combi, which is a combined passenger/freighter with a side cargo door. Unlike the -200C, however, only a matter of hours are required to alter the fit in a Combi, and the operator can adjust the ratio of seats/cargo space to suit the requirements for individual flights. An internal dividing wall separates passengers from the cargo area, and as this wall is usually painted in the same decor as the rest of the cabin – in most cases passengers are probably unaware of the cargo compartment behind them. The first -200 Combi, registration C-GAGA, was the 250th 747 built, and was delivered to Air Canada in March 1975. The 500th 'Jumbo' was also a -200B Combi, built this time for Scandinavian Airlines System, and it was rolled out in

Right Rotate! With barely 1000 ft of Gatwick's 10,364 ft-long runway left, heavily-laden British Airways 747-236B G-BDXJ *City of Birmingham* lifts off at the start of an eight-hour/forty-minute flight to Bridgetown, Barbados

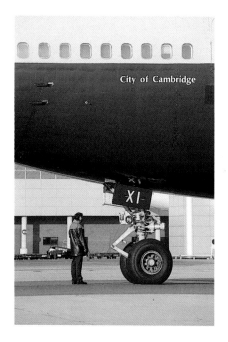

Above With the push back completed safely, the tow-bar is quickly disconnected. Meanwhile, up in the cockpit the captain checks with the ground engineer, via an intercom, that everything is 'OK' prior to taxy clearance being granted from the tower. This shot amply demonstrates the sheer size of the 747, with a good comparison being made between the nose gear wheel and the engineer – I'm glad I don't have to buy tyres that size for my car!

Right The cockpit of a 747-200, when compared to the -400, looks distinctly dated and old-fashioned, with a multitude of analogue instruments – just the thought of having to monitor all those dials during a a long-haul flight is enough to give you eye-strain

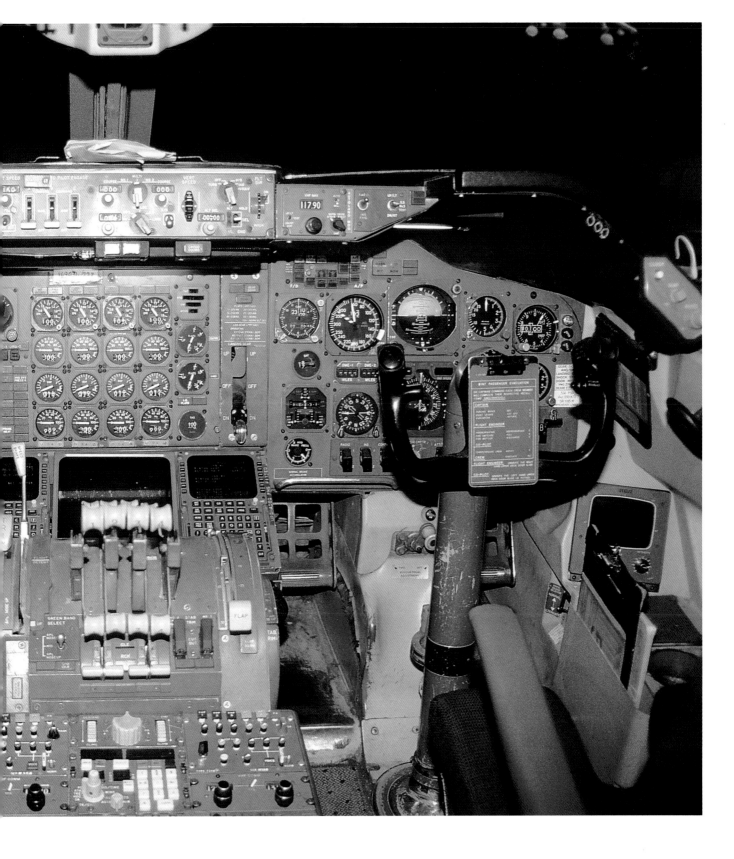

Left During overhaul and servicing nothing is left to chance. Here, an engineer checks the fan blades of a Rolls-Royce RB211-524D4 engine fitted to a British Airways 747-236

Above It was a sad day in British aviation history when the 'David' of the industry, British Caledonian, finally succumbed to the British Airways 'Goliath' and was gobbled up in December 1987. Sadly the British Government refused to intervene as BA sought to increase its monopoly, a situation which was tragically allowed to occur again more recently with the demise of Dan-Air. At the time of the take over British Caledonian was operating BAC 111s on domestic and European routes, and DC-10s and 747s on services to the US, Africa, Hong Kong and Tokyo. All these aircraft were absorbed into the BA fleet, but the 747s were soon disposed of due to their incompatability with the rest of the airline's 'Jumbos'. The aircraft illustrated at Gatwick is 747-2D3B Combi G-HUGE, which was christened *Andrew Carnegie – The Scottish Philanthropist*. This jet began its career as JY-AFB of Alia - Royal Jordanian Airlines, but has now been converted to a freighter and is currently in service with Cargolux

November 1980 and delivered the following February.

To increase capacity Boeing came up with the idea of increasing the size of the upper deck, with the 'hump' being extended by some seven metres (23 ft). Japan Air Lines have two SR variants with this extension, whilst KLM returned ten of its -200Bs and -200 Combis to Boeing to have this modification incorporated. The French carrier UTA also had a pair of aircraft similarly modified. This variant is officially designated as the -200(SUD), the letters standing for 'Stretched Upper Deck'. Boeing then decided to produce its next variant with the stretched upper deck as standard, hence the Series 300 was born.

The first Boeing 747-200 to be lost was KLM's PH-BUF in the now infamous Tenerife catastrophe of 27 March 1977, which is still the world's worst air disaster. Like many such incidents, a whole sequence of events led to this tragedy. The aircraft involved should not have been at Tenerife in the first place, but had diverted there because of the closure of their intended destination of Las Palmas due to a bomb explosion. In foggy conditions, and after garbled and vague R/T instructions from Tenerife air traffic control, the KLM pilot mistakenly thought that take-off clearance had been given. It hadn't, and as his jet built up speed on its take-off roll, out of the murk loomed a Pan Am 747 taxying across the runway.

In the ensuing fireball no less than 583 people lost their lives, though, amazingly, 52 passengers and 9 crew on the Pan Am aircraft survived. Air India and Korean Air have also lost a pair of Series 200 aircraft each, all in vastly different circumstances. Air India's first crash occurred on 1 January 1978 when VT-EBD suffered an instrument failure and dived into the sea soon after take-off from Bombay, killing all 213 on board. The airline's second loss was to VT-EFO on 23 June 1985, which saw all 329 on board perish. This aircraft crashed into the sea off the south west coast of Ireland after a bomb planted by Sikh extremists at Toronto Airport exploded and literally ripped the tail off the 747.

Korean Air's first loss was HL7445 which crashed short of the runway at Seoul on 18 November 1980, but thankfully on this occasion only 14 of the 212 on board lost their lives. The airline's second crash was the well-

Right Richard Branson's Virgin Atlantic Airways began operations in June 1984 with a single 747 operating a low cost scheduled service from Gatwick to New York (Newark). The airline has steadily expanded ever since, and now operates a fleet of eight 'Jumbos', and has recently taken delivery of three of the four brand new Airbus A340s on order. Over the years the airline has deservedly won accolades for its standard of in-flight service, and has just been nominated best transatlantic airline for the third year running – quite a feat for a fledgling operator which has proved a veritable thorn in the side of state flag carrier, British Airways. Illustrated is 747-238B G-VJFK

publicised shoot-down of HL7442 over Sakhalin Island on 1 September 1983 by the Soviet Air Force after the aircraft had strayed off course and passed over defence installations in the Pacific rim region.

One aircraft which almost came to grief was British Airways G-BDXH *City of Edinburgh* when, on 24 June 1982 whilst cruising at 37,000 ft on a night flight from Kuala Lumpur to Perth, the aircraft flew through a cloud of volcanic ash spewed forth from Mt Galunggung, in Indonesia, following a huge eruption. The ash clogged the intakes of all four engines, and as the aircraft lost power it glided down to 13,000 ft before the anxious crew manage to re-start the engines one by one – unbelievably, a similar incident happened to a Singapore Airlines 747 less than a month later!

Production of the Series 200 has now ceased, and including freighter variants, 393 were built, of which over 350 are still in service.

Above As Los Angeles is served by Virgin, it was perhaps inevitable that the registration G-VLAX would be allocated to one of the airline's 747s. The aircraft in question is named *California Girl*, and like sister-ship G-VJFK, is a former Qantas 747-238B. It is illustrated here executing a perfect landing on Gatwick's runway 08R

Left All of Virgin's 747s carry personalised registrations, many of which are related to the destinations served. Seen on final approach to Heathrow from New York's John F Kennedy airport is 747-238B G-VJFK. This aircraft is allocated the name *Boston Belle*, although this sobriquet wasn't present when this shot was taken in December 1992

Above An anonymous Virgin 747 sets off into the winter sunset on another transatlantic flight from Gatwick. The airline's 'Jumbo' fleet currently comprises one 747-100 (G-VMIA) and seven Series 200s, whose personalised registrations and names are G-VMIA *Spirit of Sir Freddie*, G-TKYO *Maiden Japan*, G-VGIN *Scarlet Lady*, G-VIRG *Maiden Voyager*, G-VJFK *Boston Belle*, G-VLAX *California Girl*, G-VOYG *Shady Lady* and G-VRGN *Maid of Honour*, and a brand new Series 400. The airline took delivery of the latter, registered G-VFAB, in late April 1994, and put it to use on the Gatwick–Orlando route the following month

Left Climbing out of Gatwick into uncharacteristically clear blue skies is 747-243B G-VGIN *Scarlet Lady*. This aircraft joined Virgin in January 1986 after having served with Alitalia as I-DEMU – it also spent several periods on lease to a variety of airlines whilst owned by the Italian flag carrier. As those who have flown with the airline will testify, the standard of service is extremely high – what other operator serves tubs of ice cream to eat whilst viewing the in-flight films!

Above left Continental Airlines have recently introduced a new livery, although in my view it is nowhere near as imaginative as the airline's previous distinctive colour scheme. Although one of America's major domestic carriers, Continental has only a limited number of international routes, which are operated by a small fleet of DC-10-30s and 747s. The 'Jumbo' fleet comprises only eight aircraft – two Series 100s and six -200s, all of which are second-hand. N33021 is a 747-243B which previously served with Alitalia, Qantas and People Express

Left A puff of smoke marks the spot where Continental's N78019 made initial contact with the Gatwick runway

following the successful completion of yet another transatlantic flight. This particular aircraft is no stranger to Gatwick, having previously been based at the airport as G-BJXN of British Caledonian. It is a 747-230B, and was originally delivered to Lufthansa in 1972 as D-ABYG, before serving with Braniff as N611BN. When the aircraft was absorbed into the British Airways fleet it received the name *City of Worcester*, though this was short-lived as the jet was sold in May 1990 to Potomac Capital Investment Corporation, from whom it is leased by Continental

Above Lift off! A Northwest Airlines 747-251B takes-off from Gatwick

Above left Looking in absolutely immaculate condition as it lifts off from runway 24R at Toronto's Lester B Pearson International airport is Alitalia 747-243B I-DEMN *Portocervo*. This aircraft was delivered in November 1981, and is one of 14 Series 200s operated by the Italian flag carrier

Left Skimming over the rooftops of Kowloon on short finals to runway 13 at Hong Kong's Kai Tak airport is Alitalia's 747-243B Combi I-DEMW *Spoleto*. Alitalia now uses a small fleet of recently delivered McDonnell-Douglas MD-11s to supplement the 747s on long-haul routes, including the Rome–Hong Kong service

Above Lufthansa was the premier European carrier to operate the 747, receiving its first 747-130 in February 1970. Only three of this variant were delivered to the airline, which chose instead to concentrate on the Series 230, 19 of which are currently in service. The bulk of these are -230B Combis, although a few freighters are also in use – indeed, Lufthansa was the first airline to operate a freighter variant. Photographed about to land at Kai Tak is -230B D-ABZD *Kiel*

Above Olympic Airways operates a fleet of four Series 200 'Jumbos', one of which was delivered new in 1973 – the other three are former Singapore Airlines machines bought in 1984/85. One of the latter is 747-212B SX-OAD *Olympic Flame*, which was photographed in the airline's new livery in March 1993 at Sydney's Kingsford-Smith International airport

Above right Martinair Holland operates three Series 200 'Jumbos', one of which is a dedicated freighter, whilst the other two are Combis. The latter are generally used in the passenger role during the summer, but converted into freighters for the winter months. Photographed operating a cargo run into Hong Kong in December 1987 is 747-21AC Combi PH-MCE *Prins van Oranje*. This aircraft was delivered to Martinair from the Everett production line as late as February 1987

Right The current El Al fleet consists entirely of Boeing products, comprising 757s, 767s and 747s, as well as a couple of 737s, which are leased to the domestic airline Arkia. The 'Jumbo' fleet comprises seven Series 200s, one of which is a freighter, and a single -100F. The airline also has two 747-400s on order for delivery in 1994. Photographed inbound to London's Heathrow airport is 747-258B 4X-AXB, which has served the airline continuously since it was delivered new to the Israeli flag carrier in November 1971

Above left Middle East Airlines (MEA) of Lebanon currently has three 747-2B4B Combis in serice. These aircraft were delivered new to MEA during 1975, but due to the civil war that then gripped the country, the airline had no real use for them, and they were subsequently sold to an American leasing company. These aircraft have seen periods of service with a number of airlines over the ensuing 19 years, although all three are presently under lease to their former owners! N202AE was originally registered OD-AGH, and is seen here on approach to Paris/Orly in August 1992

Left Prior to the Gulf War Iraqi Airways 747s were regular visitors to Heathrow. Since that event, however, the airline has all but ceased to function due to United Nations sanctions. Like the bulk of the its fleet, the three 747-270 Combis have not flown since the conflict, and will no doubt require a considerable amount of work to bring them to an airworthy condition should they enter service once again. Illustrated here at Heathrow between flights is the airline's first 747, YI-AGN, which was christened *Tigris*

Above Kuwait Airways 747 fleet comprises four Series 269B Combi aircraft, the first of which was delivered in July 1978. These jets are used on routes to London and New York, and in 1995 will be supplemented by three - 469 Combis. The 747 illustrated here is the airline's fourth 'Jumbo', 9K-ADD *Al Salmiya*, which entered service in January 1982. This photograph was taken in February 1989, and since the Gulf War some aircraft have had a yellow ribbon with the slogan, 'Don't forget our PoWs', painted on them – more recently a slightly revised livery has also been noted

Above Air Gabon, the state airline of the former French colony, operates a modest number of jets from its Libreville base. The pride of the fleet is the company's sole Boeing 747-2Q2B Combi, which is used on the Paris service. The aircraft was delivered on 16 July 1978 and, although allocated the registration TR-LXK, has never worn these marks, wearing F-ODJG instead – this registration is actually reserved for French overseas colonies. The aircraft carries the name *President Leon Mba* on the nose, and was photographed under tow at Paris/Charles de Gaulle airport in August 1992

Above right The flying springbok logo of South African Airways (SAA) as adorned the tail of 747s since October 1971, when ZS-SAN, the first of seven Series 200 jets, was delivered – the airline has since taken delivery of six 747SPs, two -300s and four -400s. Due to SAA's location in the southern part of the African continent, the 747 has proved to be the ideal aircraft for the airline, and the type performs virtually all the company's intercontinental routes. In this photograph, 747-244B ZS-SAO *Magaliesberg* is seen just moments away from touchdown at Kai Tak following a long over-water haul from Johannesburg

Right Air India was the second Asian airline to order the 747, and they used it to replace 707s initially on the London and New York routes. Due to the interior finish, and distinctive paintwork around the windows, the Air India 'Jumbos' were described as 'Palaces in the Sky'. In late 1989 the airline introduced a new livery which dispensed with the 'Palace' image, but they were unprepared for the furore which ensued as religious leaders, and the Indian population as a whole, demanded the return of their 'Palaces'! The strength of feeling was such that the airline has since relented, and the new -400s which have just been delivered are in the operator's old livery – complete with 'Palace' windows. Showing those to good effect here is 747-237B VT-EGC *Harsha Vardhana*

Above The national airline of India's neighbour, and long time foe, is also a 747 operator. Pakistan International Airlines currently has eight Series 200Bs in its inventory, including two former TAP and four former Canadian Pacific machines. The aircraft illustrated here, however, is one of a pair of -240B Combis which were delivered new to the airline in 1979/80. AP-BAK was photographed at the point of rotation from runway 24L at Amsterdam's Schiphol airport as flight PK714 to Karachi

Above right An airline which has seen tremendous growth over the past decade is Thai Airways International. Regional and intercontinental routes are undertaken by Airbus A300s, McDonnell-Douglas MD-11s and Boeing 747s. The latter fleet comprises six Series 200s, two -300s and seven -400s, with a further five -400s on order. Thai's first 747, the 402nd 'Jumbo' built, was delivered in November 1979. Photographed at Auckland airport in February 1993 is 747-2D7B HS-TGG, named *Sriwanna*

Right The 'Jumbo' has proved to be a very popular aircraft with Asia's international airlines, most of whom have a few in their inventory. Philippine Airlines commenced 747 operations in January 1980 with a Manila–Honolulu–San Francisco service. America remains the airline's strongest market, though 747s are also used on European routes. The airline initially received four -2F6B variants, although over the years the numbers in the 747 fleet have fluctuated somewhat as aircraft were leased from other operators. Currently, in 1994, it numbers ten -200s and two -400s, the latter being delivered at the end of 1993. Photographed poised for a landing at Gatwick is 747-283B Combi EI-BTS. This aircraft was the 500th 'Jumbo' built and was delivered to SAS in February 1981. Now Irish-registered, it belongs to Guiness-Peat Aviation, from whom it has been leased since February 1988

Another Asian carrier with an ever increasing fleet of Boeing aircraft is Malaysia Airlines. The company received its first 747s in 1982 when it was known as Malaysian Airlines System, these taking the form of two -236Bs ordered by British Airways but not taken up. A few years later a single Series 3H6 Combi was purchased, and over the past decade another nine 4H6 Combi models have entered service, with four more on order. Climbing out of Amsterdam's Schiphol airport into a cloudless sky is the airline's first 747, 9M-MHI

Malaysia's near neighbour is the tiny island nation of Singapore, yet, despite its size, the national airline has the second largest 747 fleet in the world with no less than 62 aircraft on strength, or on order – more than any US operator! Singapore Airlines boasts one of the youngest fleets of any carrier too, and some of its earlier 747s were sold off after only six years service following their replacement with newer aircraft. Of the 19 -212Bs originally operated by the airline, only a few remain, with the series -312 'Big Top' and -412 'Megatop' accounting for the majority of their burgeoning fleet. Photographed after take-off from runway 31 at Kai Tak airport is 747-212B 9V-SQL – this aircraft was delivered new to the airline in February 1980, but was disposed of in 1989, and in its current guise flies as G-VRGN of Virgin Atlantic

Above The current Garuda Indonesia livery was introduced in 1986, and features a Garuda bird in various shades of turquoise on a dark blue fin. The airline has operated 747s since 1980, and over a two-year period six 747-2U3Bs were delivered. These are frequently supplemented by additional leased aircraft for the annual Hadj pilgrimage to Jeddah. In January 1994 Garuda took delivery of the first of nine -400 variants, and no doubt it will not be long before the earlier -200s are disposed of. Illustrated here is 747-2U3B PK-GSD taxying for departure as flight GA977 to Jakarta

Right Garuda 747-2U3B PK-GSF taxying to its parking position at Zurich. The weather conditions leave something to be desired, and are not what one expects of a July afternoon in Switzerland

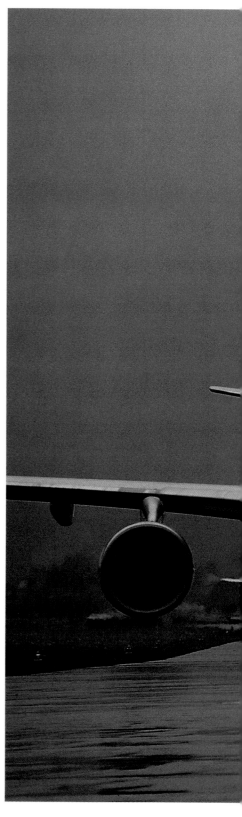

Left The approach to runway 13 at Hong Kong's Kai Tak is without a doubt one of the most interesting and demanding in the world. Due to the daunting terrain – primarily a mountain named Lion Rock – a standard ILS (Instrument Landing System) approach is not possible. Therefore, aircraft make a modified ILS approach, known as an IGS (Instrument Guidance System), which terminates at the foot of the mountain – Lion Rock is liberally daubed with large red and white squares, so as to increase its visiblity. At a pre-determined point the pilot has to take-over visually and, at one-third of a mile from touchdown, executes a 47° turn. The sight of a 'Jumbo' making such a manoeuvre just a few hundred feet over crowded Kowloon is quite something!

Above The first 'Jumbo' acquired by Cathay Pacific was Series 267B VR-HKG in July 1979. The airline has come a long way since then, and now has a fleet of 37 747s in use, or on order. Most of these are Series 400 aircraft, but six -300s and eleven -200s still give sterling service, with four of the latter in use as freighters. Pioneering Cathay 747 VR-HKG is seen here about to make a perfect landing at Kai Tak

Above The days of Chinese airlines operating inefficient and unreliable Soviet-built aircraft are virtually a thing of the past now, and an ever-increasing number of fledgling outfits seem to be queueing at 'Mr. Boeing's' door in a rush to hand over their dollars in exchange for the latest in Western airliner technology. Only a decade ago things were so different, with only one airline, CAAC (Civil Aviation Administration of China), which was also the regulatory body, waving the flag for the world's most populous nation The airline then operated mostly Soviet equipment, and Boeing was only just getting a foot in the door. One of the first examples of the CAAC turning westward in search of civil hardware was 747-2J6B Combi B-2450, which was photographed seconds away from landing at Kai Tak in April 1987

Right Japan Air Lines boasts the world's largest 747 fleet, with an incredible 94 aircraft in service, or on order, no less than 40 of which are Series 400 jets. The airline also has three -300 aircraft on lease from Qantas, which are flown by Australian flight deck crews and Japanese cabin attendants for use on the lucrative Tokyo–Sydney route. The airline has, and still does, operate every variant of the 747 apart from the SP. The older Series 100 aircraft have virtually disappeared from the fleet, but large numbers of -200s still soldier on. Executing the 47° turn on final approach to runway 13 at Kai Tak is 747-246B JA8114

Above The scheme worn by Air New Zealand's 747-219B ZK-NZZ is definitely non-standard. This photograph was taken at Auckland in February 1993 when the aircraft had just returned from a period of lease with Malaysia Airlines, hence its rudimentary scheme. Air New Zealand operates five -219Bs and three -419s

Left In 1990 Japan Air Lines introduced a new livery which placed an increasing emphasis on an all-white fuselage – this rather boring corporate trend has steadily spread through the world's airlines over the past five years. Showing the new scheme to full effect on the taxyway at Honolulu is 747-246B JA8111. This aircraft is now over 20 years old, having originally been delivered to JAL in March 1972

Abcve The Central and South American continent boasts fewer 747s than any other region in the world, with only Argentinian, Brazilian and Colombian airlines currently operating the type. Aerolineas Argentinas runs a fleet of six 747-287Bs, which were procured between 1979 and 1982. Illustrated about to line up on runway 09R at Heathrow for the flight to Buenos Aires is LV-OOZ

Above right Having initially acquired 747-100s, the purchase of the Series 200 was a logical progression for Air Canada, and they currently operate a modest fleet of three Combis. The first was the 250th 'Jumbo' built, and it was delivered to the airline in March 1975, with a second following in 1979. The third, however, was acquired almost a decade later in January 1988 from Qantas, with whom it was registered VH-ECA. This aircraft is seen at Heathrow wearing its present registration of C-GAGC

Right One of the great pioneers of Canadian aviation was Max Ward, who founded his own company, Wardair, in 1952. By the time his first 747 was acquired in April 1973 Wardair was an established charter operator, and this aircraft was used on transatlantic flights in the summer and to Florida and the Caribbean in the winter. Wardair eventually operated a total of five 'Jumbos' – three Series 100s and two -200s. Sadly, the airline ceased to function in 1990 after being taken over by Canadian Airlines International. Photographed at Toronto in October 1985 is 747-211B C-GXRA, this aircraft having been delivered new in 1978 to Wardair, who in turn leased it to Libyan Arab Airlines on two separate occasions before it was bought outright by British Caledonian, with whom it operated as G-GLYN

B747F
CARGO VARIANTS

The design of the 747 makes the type an ideal freighter, and from the outset this was one of the tasks the design team had in mind for the 'Jumbo'. However, when the first Series 100 aircraft entered service there was no engine available with sufficient thrust to enable Boeing to produce such a dedicated version. Later in the 747's lifespan when more powerful engines became available, a number of surplus -100s were 'up-engined' and modified into freighters. This involved removing all the seats and other items such as galleys, toilets, over-head lockers and the like usually associated with a long-haul passenger airliner. A hole would then be cut in the side of the fuselage and a side cargo door door installed. In addition, the main deck floor was strengthened.

The first dedicated freighter variant was the -200F, which was based on the -200B – it was instantly recognisable by the lack of windows in the main cabin. An innovative feature was the upward hinging nose which opens to allow outsize cargo and pallets to be loaded easily, whilst a side cargo door was available as an option allowing simultaneous loading/unloading. To assist this process, a mechanised cargo handling system, which included rollers along the floor of the main deck, was fitted as standard, thus allowing just two men to load or unload a whole aircraft in just 30 minutes – or so the Boeing advert said! In addition, there was still room in the hold under the floor for pallets or stowed cargo.

The first -200F was ordered by Lufthansa, who duly took delivery of the aircraft on 9 March 1972 and christened it *Cargonaut*. This jet could carry a maximum payload of 118,000 kg (260,000 lb) nearly 3000 miles. Surprisingly

Right The hustle and bustle of an army of ground handlers moving about with dozens of cargo containers surround this Northwest 747F as it is loaded in the cargo terminal at Kai Tak. The airport boasts one of the highest turn-round rates of cargo, with virtually every freighter movement being operated by 747Fs. The aircraft featured, 747-251F(SCD) N639US was photographed at Kai Tak in August 1987, just two months after it had been delivered

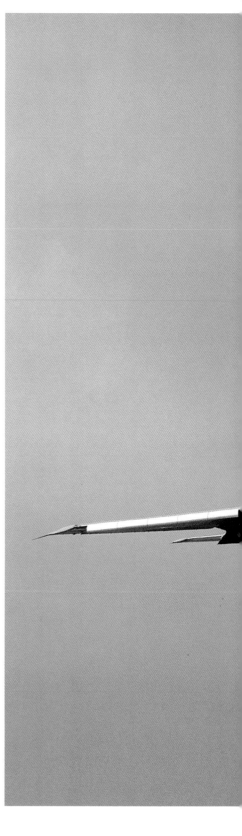

sales of the -200F proved very slow indeed, and for two years Lufthansa remained the sole operator. In the latter half of 1974 Japan Air Lines, Seaboard World and Air France also received -200Fs, and US airlines also began to show a healthy interest in the type, which eventually resulted in both Flying Tigers and Northwest Orient ordering the variant. Air France nicknamed their -200Fs *Super Pelicans*, the upward opening door no doubt being responsible for this piece of inspirational thinking!

The Imperial Iranian Air Force operated a fleet of four -200Fs and a larger number of -100Fs, all of which have since been disposed of. As described earlier, under the Series -200 designation, the -200C convertible passenger/freighter is also fitted with the opening nose, and is frequently operated as a pure cargo carrier. For instance, the Dutch airline Martinair generally uses the -200C as a freighter in winter and as a passenger hauler in summer. The 67th, and last, -200F built was delivered to Air France in October 1991.

With more powerful and fuel efficient engines on offer a freighter variant of the Series 400 was inevitable. Air France was the first to order the

Above Looking its age, Northwest's N639US lands at Kai Tak after a transpacific flight from Seattle. This aircraft had only been in service a mere eight weeks when this photograph was taken on 12 August 1987

Right The black and white nose cone somehow adds to the immaculate shine of the natural metal surfaces of Northwest's 747-251F(SCD) N639US

-400F, although Cargolux actually introduced the new type into service in November 1993. The -400F is capable of transporting a 113,000 kg (249,000 lb) payload a distance of 8100 km (4400 nm), and Cargolux estimates that the increased range will permit the carrier to dispense with around 300 refuelling stops a year. The Luxembourg-based airline currently has two -400Fs, with a third on order for delivery in 1996/97, and options on a further three. The saving in airport handling charges alone is significant, and as the -400F does not carry passengers there is no stretched upper deck, nor, surprisingly, are there any winglets fitted – in fact, its external appearance is virtually identical to the much older -200F.

Above Climbing away from the runway at Osan Air Base, Republic of Korea, is Flying Tigers 747 EI-BPH, which at the time was on lease from Guiness-Peat

Right Flying Tigers were synonymous with air freight for a very long time, but the once-dominant US cargo operator was taken over by Federal Express in 1989. Photographed inbound to the world's 747 freighter hub – Kai Tak – is 747-121F(SCD) N817FT. This jet started its life as N654PA, a Pan Am 747-121, before being converted to a Side Cargo Door configuration early in 1977. During its life with Pan Am it bore two different names – *Clipper White Wing* and *Clipper Pacific Trader*. It was sold to Flying Tigers in February 1983, and after only a brief period of service with Federal Express, was again sold on in 1991 to United Parcel Service, with whom it currently serves as N682UP

A busy scene at Tokyo's Narita airport as 747 freighters of Evergreen and Japan Air Lines are unloaded, whilst a conventional Malaysia 747-200 airliner receives attention prior to receiving its 'self-loading' cargo *(Toshiki Kudo)*

Above Evergreen International Airlines operates a scheduled freighter network across the globe. It has also received many US Government contracts for military re-supplying of overseas bases, and its aircraft are frequent visitors to USAF facilities in Europe and the Far East. Its fleet comprises DC-8s, DC-9s, Boeing 727s and 747s, with the latter being the most numerous of all four types. Its 'Jumbo' fleet comprises a mixed bag of Series 100s and -200s, Combis and freighters, including several ex-Pan Am machines. Illustrated here about to land at Heathrow is 747-132(SCD) N479EV. This jet previously served with Delta, China Airlines and Pan American, and was converted to Combi configuration in 1986

Above right Korean Air have without a doubt one of the most imaginative liveries around, a scheme which extends to their cargo fleet. The sky blue fuselage colour even encompasses the whole fin, upon which is painted a large 'Taeguk' – the national insignia. Seen on its take-off roll from runway 13 at Kai Tak is 747-2B5F(SCD) HL7452, which was delivered to the airline in June 1980

Right Operating a large fleet of passenger-configured 'Jumbos' in the first place, it was inevitable that Singapore Airlines would also employ the freighter variant, and the airline currently has three -200 freighters, with two -400 freighters on order. Of the Series 200s, one was acquired new in 1988, whilst the remaining aircraft are more recent additions, being former Federal Express aircraft which were delivered to Singapore in 1992. Series -245F(SCD) 9V-SQU was one of the latter, and it was photographed rotating from runway 24L at Schiphol soon after its purchase

Above There is a considerable amount if trade done between the Republic of China (Taiwan) and Hong Kong, and although the bulk of it is moved by sea, there are frequent 747 freighter flights between the territories. China Airlines presently operates three -200Fs, although they did have a fourth. This aircraft was 747-2R7F B-198, which was acquired from Cargolux in 1985. Unfortunately it was destroyed when it crashed soon after take-off from Taipei on 29 December 1991, killing the crew. Here, it is photographed in happier times about to land at Kai Tak in December 1987

Above right Air Hong Kong was founded in 1986 and began operations soon afterwards with a Boeing 707

freighter. The airline has since upgraded to the 747F, of which it has three, including 747-132F(SCD) VR-HKN. This aircraft had previously served with Delta, Flying Tigers and Federal Express, and was photographed during a scheduled service to Manchester's Ringway airport

Right As the world's largest 747 operator it comes as no surprise that Japan Air Lines operates ten Series 200 freighters, although, rather unusually, the operator has no plans at present to acquire the freighter variant of the -400. Wearing bold 'JALCARGO' titles, -246F(SCD) JA8151 was photographed about to land at Osaka in April 1990 following a long transpacific haul across from America

Above A recently formed subsidiary of Japan Air Lines is JUST - Japan Universal System Transport. The company utilises JAL's 747-221F(SCD) JA8160 primarily on flights for the parent company, hence it is a frequent visitor to locations such as Hong Kong and London. It was photographed on push-back from the cargo terminal at Narita airport *(Toshiki Kudo)*

Above right Iran Air currently operates four 747SPs, one Series 100 and two -200 Combis. It also has two pure freighters, one of which is a former Iranian Air Force machine. The jet in question is 747-2J9F EP-ICC, and it is seen here during one of its frequent visits to Heathrow

Right It is presumably for security reasons that El Al's freighter aircraft wear no titles or company logo, even though they are painted in the Israeli airline's distinctive livery. Photographed at Schiphol is 747-258C 4X-AXF, operating in the pure freighter role. This photograph was taken exactly one week before sister-ship 4X-AXG tragically crashed into an Amsterdam suburb after losing an engine on take-off

Above Cargolux is one of Europe's largest all-freight airlines and, as the name suggests, it is based in Luxembourg. It currently employs a fleet of five 747 freighters, although its aircraft frequently appear in the livery of other airlines during periods of lease. Cargolux became the first airline to receive the series -400F, and two of the three on order had been delivered by the end of 1993. Its aircraft can be seen in just about every corner of the globe, including Hong Kong, where 747-271C(SCD) LX-BCV was photographed in December 1987. This jet has obviously just returned from a spell on lease with Saudia, whose livery it still wears, although Cargolux titles and logo have also been hastily applied

Right Boeing 747-2B3F F-GBOX is one of two freighter variants which have been operated by the French airline UTA (Union de Transports Aeriens) for many years. This aircraft was delivered in August 1979, and was photographed at Kai Tak operating an Air France service. Its sister ship, F-GPAN, was sold to Air France in 1986, although they were recently 're-united' once again following the sale of UTA to the French national flag carrier

B747SP

One variant which is instantly recognisable is the 747SP, the acronym standing for 'Special Performance'. Although it shares 90 per cent commonality of components with the Series 100 and -200, the aircraft has had its fuselage length reduced by some 14.35 m (47 ft 1 in), giving it a somewhat stumpy appearance. The tail fin is slightly taller in height and the tailplane's span increased by some 3.05 m (10 ft). The jet's passenger capacity was obviously reduced by these drastic modifications, usually to about 331 in a three-class configuration, although in an all-economy fit up to 440 could be carried. The *raison d'être* of the SP was its long range, although its higher cruising speed and reduced fuel consumption were also crucial ingredients that made it an ideal aircraft for 'thin' long-haul routes.

The 747SP was announced in August 1973, and within weeks that great pioneering airline, Pan Am, had ordered ten of these new machines. The first SP, and 265th 747 built, was rolled out on 19 May 1975, with the maiden flight following on 4 July – Independence Day. The aircraft was originally registered N747SP, and along with the next three aircraft, was used for the seven-month long certification programme, during which the type undertook a worldwide tour and broke another record whilst performing a 11,289 km (7015 miles) non-stop flight from Seattle to Tokyo.

Even when the type had been in service for over a decade, the SP was still capable of 'pushing the outside of the civil airliner envelope', as it proved in January 1988 when a United Airlines jet (ex-Pan Am, flying its former owner's routes in the Pacific) completed an around-the-world trip in just 36 hours and 54 minutes flying time, routing through Seattle–Athens–Taipei–Seattle. Although orders for the SP were slow, airlines which did put the type into service included Braniff, China Airlines, CAAC, Iran Air, Korean Air, Qantas, Saudia, South African, Syrianair, and TWA.

Despite the small number in service with commercial fleet operators, the

Right The livery of United Airlines suits the stubby 'Baby Boeing' SP variant. Banking 'round the corner' onto final approach for Kai Tak's runway 13 in December 1987 is N144UA, which had previously served with Pan American as N534PA *Clipper Great Republic*

SP has, however, proved popular as a VIP executive transport aircraft, and the governments of Iraq, Oman, Saudi Arabia and the United Arab Emirates utilise the aircraft in this role. More recent operators include fledgling airlines such as Air Namibia and Tajikistan Air, who operate aircraft leased from South African and United respectively. An attractive and photogenic aircraft, the SP remained in production for a short time only, before the line was closed in August 1982. Only 44 were built, although one further aircraft was delivered to the United Arab Emirates Government in 1987.

Above United plans to dispose of its 747SPs in the near future, so it came as something of a surprise to airliner aficionados when N145UA appeared at Heathrow in the operator's new livery in June 1993. United have currently leased one SP to newly formed Tajik Air, who use the aircraft on a Dushanbe–Heathrow service – this enterprising young airline hope to acquire a second aircraft from the same source to inaugurate a Los Angeles service

Right This photograph of a United SP in hybrid markings was taken in April 1986, shortly after the company purchased Pan American's Pacific routes and some of its aircraft, including TriStars and 747SPs. The aircraft's Pan Am livery has been removed and replaced by a hastily-applied United logo and titles. Note that the aircraft still wears its former Pan Am registration, N531PA. This was Pan Am's second 747SP-21, and it was delivered to the airline in May 1976 and named *Clipper Freedom*. It was re-registered N141UA in September 1986

Above left Photographed in an unusual, but anonymous, livery is 747SP-31 N57202. This machine was delivered to TWA in March 1980, but was sold only four years later to aircraft brokers Jet Aviation. It appeared in Hong Kong in mid-1986, where it was destined for VIP conversion prior to delivery to the Brunei Government, but this failed contract failed to materialise and the SP was ultimately sold to American Airlines as N601AA

Left An early customer for the SP variant was South African Airways, who received a total of six aircraft, although none of these are presently used by the airline. One was sold to Royal Air Maroc in 1986, whilst the remaining five are still owned by SAA, but leased to other carriers; two each to Air Mauritius and Air Namibia and one to Luxair. South Africa's aircraft have the airline's titles in English on the port side and in Afrikaans on the starboard, as seen on 747SP-44 ZS-SPE *Hantam,* photographed on the taxyway at Kai Tak

Above Iran Air took delivery of four SP-86 variants in the 1970s, all of which are still in service. The first two arrived in March and May of 1976 respectively, with the third following a year later and the fourth in 1979. The type still operates the airline's Teheran–London route, and EP-IAC *Fars* was photographed about to land at Heathrow at the end of a flight from the Middle East

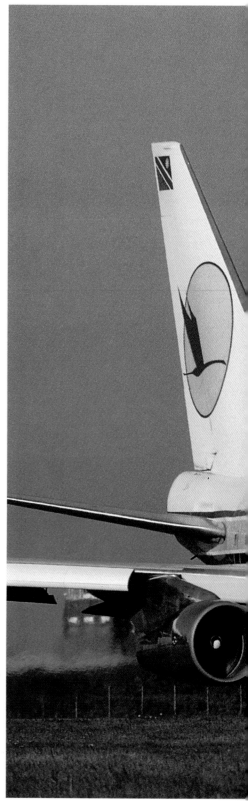

Above Namibia boasts its own international airline which operates services from Windhoek, including a twice-weekly service to London/Heathrow. The latter service is operated by a 747SP-44 leased from South African Airways, but in full Air Namibia livery. The aircraft illustrated is Air Namibia's first 747SP-44, V5-SPF *Etosha*, and it was photographed in June 1993 lining-up on runway 09R at Heathrow for an 1845 departure as flight SW682. The airline's only other jet equipment is a 737-200, which is used on regional services, whilst a few Beech 1900s are also employed on internal routes

Right Air Namibia has found its Windhoek–Heathrow service to be both popular and profitable over the past few years, so much so that a second 747SP – V5-SPE – was acquired from the same source in March 1993

Easily identifiable due to the satellite communications equipment housed in a purpose-built dorsal hump, the 747SP used by the Omani Government as a VIP aircraft is kept in immaculate condition. This jet was the 405th 'Jumbo' built, and was initially delivered to Braniff Airways in October 1979. After only five years service it was bought by the Omanis, although the conversion to bring it to its present standard took three long years to complete – much longer than it took to build the SP in the first place! It is operated by the Royal Flight of Oman, who have recently doubled their fleet following the acquisition of a former United Airlines SP. The ruler of the nearby State of Dubai also has a 747SP; in this case a former TWA machine. Wearing the national colours of Oman, 747SP-31 A40-SO was photographed at the start of its take-off run at Heathrow

Although China Airlines operated the 747-200 series from Taipei to Los Angeles, the aircraft required a technical stop at Honolulu en route. However, with the advent of the SP variant, the airline could offer a non-stop service to the West Coast of the USA, with San Francisco being the chosen destination – four SPs were purchased for this and a Taipei–Anchorage–New York route. With the introduction of the MD-11 and 747-400, the SPs have become somewhat surplus to requirements. However, rather than dispose of them, China Airlines have handed three of the four over to subsidiary company Mandarin Airlines. Illustrated being loaded and replenished at Taipei's Chiang Kai Shek International airport is 747SP-09 N4508H

Above The airline of the 'other' China, the People's Republic, used to be CAAC, and their first order with Boeing for 'Jumbos' consisted of three SP variants, which were duly delivered in 1980, with a fourth, second-hand, machine following in late 1982. These aircraft were predominantly used on services to Europe, including Zurich, where B-2454 was photographed in August 1989

Right Over the last few years CAAC has ceased to exist as an operating airline, although it is still the regulatory body for aviation in the People's Republic of China. This giant landmass has seen a virtual explosion of new airlines in almost every corner of the vast country, and the 747SPs are now operated by Air China, the country's new flag carrier. Climbing steeply out of Gatwick, and still wearing CAAC livery, is 747SP-J6 B-2442. This shot perfectly illustrates the stubby lines of the 'Baby Boeing'

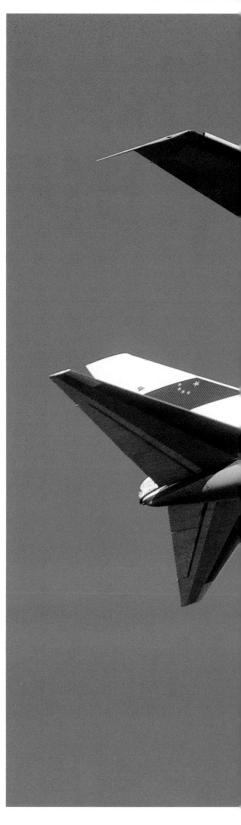

B747-300

The next variant produced after the 747SP was the Series -300, which featured the Stretched Upper Deck as standard – otherwise the dimensions mirrored that of the -200. Internally, the distinctive spiral staircase to the upper deck was replaced by a straight staircase, allowing the capacity of this section to be increased to 69, whilst additional emergency exits were added to cope with the increased numbers. The Stretched Upper Deck feature had both good and bad points to it. On the positive side, the aerodynamics were improved by the streamlined shape, resulting in a slight increase in airspeed from Mach 0.84 to 0.85. This advantage, however, was more than evened out by the resulting increase in weight to the tune of some 9000 lb, which resulted in the maximum range being reduced by 2695 km (1674 miles)! This was the main reason why sales of the -300 were so poor in comparison to those achieved with the -200.

The first 747-300 was rolled out on 15 September 1982, this Combi version being delivered to Swissair as HB-IGC. This was the 570th 'Jumbo' to leave the Everett production line, and its maiden flight took place on 5 October – due to the certification programme, the aircraft wasn't delivered until 19 March 1983. The normal capacity for the -300 is 538 passengers, but Japan Air Lines were quick to capitalise on this by acquiring an SR variant with a capacity of 563!

Other customers for the Series 300 included Cathay Pacific, Egyptair, KLM, Korean Air, Malaysian, Qantas, Sabena, Saudia, Singapore, South African, Thai, UTA and Varig. The Series 300s of Singapore Airlines are dubbed 'BIG TOPS', and this logo is painted on the forward upper fuselage. The airline has continued in the same vein with its -400s, which are known as 'MEGATOPS'. The first, and so far only, loss of a 747-300 befell UTA's F-GDUA, which was severely damaged by fire whilst under maintenance at Paris Charles de Gaulle airport on 16 March 1985 and was

Right The most obvious difference between the Boeing 747-300 and the earlier Series 100s and -200s is the Stretched Upper Deck. Despite the increase in passenger capacity the -300 has been the least popular full-size variant as far as the airlines are concerned. There are currently 15 operators utilising the -300 worldwide, including Cathay Pacific who boast a fleet of six aircraft

subsequently declared a write-off. Ironically, as these words are written a new Air France A340 has just suffered the same fate at the same location!

Production of the -300 ceased in 1990, with the last aircraft being delivered to Sabena. A mere 80 were built overall, and 79 of these are still in service.

Above As an operator of the Series 200, upgrading to the -300 was a logical step for Thai Airlines, although only two aircraft were acquired, both in December 1987. Photographed at its Bangkok base on 3 January 1988 after having been in service for exactly one month is 747-3D7 HS-TGE *Chutamat*. Thai operates its 747-300s in an 18/62/325 seat configuration

Left Another Asian operator who added the Series 300 to its fleet to supplement its -200s was Singapore Airlines. These aircraft were nicknamed 'BIG TOPS' due to their extended upper deck area, this sobriquet being painted on the forward fuselage behind the cockpit. The first of 14 such aircraft to enter service with the airline was delivered in April 1983, and the last in March 1987. These jets operate in a 20/54/340 configuration, apart from the last three delivered which are Combis. Although allocated Singaporean registrations, many of the aircraft are American-registered – the two-letter portion of the US registration corresponds with the last two letters of its Singapore registration! One such aircraft is N119KE, which is also allocated 9V-SKE, and was photographed about to land at Kai Tak

Above The Australian national airline Qantas is a well established Boeing operator and, along with Korean Air and South African, currently operates every variant of the 747, with the exception of the Series 100. None of the above airlines have operated -100s apart from Qantas, who have flown a few on lease from time to time. Qantas has six 747-338s, including VH-EBV *City of Geraldton*, which was photographed at Auckland en route to Sydney

Left Qantas presently operates three of its 747-338s in association with Japan Air Lines on the Tokyo–Sydney route. These aircraft operate in the full livery of JAL, who also provide the cabin crew, whilst Qantas supply the flight deck crew. One of the aircraft involved is VH-EBT *City of Wagga Wagga*, which was photographed on an unusually clear day at Kai Tak back in August 1986

Above The Brazilian national carrier Varig operates a fleet of 747-200s, -300s and -400s. Of the five -341s that began entering service almost a decade ago, the first two were Combi variants, which were delivered in December 1985, followed by three standard aircraft in April and May of 1988. The latter are used alongside the newer -400s on the Rio de Janeiro–Heathrow service, and it was at the latter location that PP-VOA was photographed in November 1993. This particular aircraft was the 701st 'Jumbo' to take to the air, and is currently on long-term lease from the International Lease Finance Corporation

Above right Saudia, the Saudi Arabian flag carrier, operates a large fleet of Boeing 737s, 747s, Airbus A300s and Lockheed L-1011 TriStars. The 747 fleet comprises every variant except the -400, which, surprisingly, the airline has yet to order, although at the time of writing a decision as to the fleet replacement programme was

imminent. The airline operates ten 747-368s on intercontinental routes, plus a further example on behalf of the Saudi Royal Family, which is in basic Saudia livery. These ten Rolls-Royce powered aircraft were delivered during 1985 and 1986, with HZ-AIT being the last to arrive on 10 November – it is is seen here at Paris/Charles de Gaulle airport in August 1992

Right Launch customer for the 747-300 was Swissair, who placed an initial order for four, all of which were delivered in 1983. A fifth example joined the airline in December 1987, and all of them are still on strength, three being Combi aircraft. These aircraft are used primarily on services to the US, with MD-11s performing flights mainly to Asia and South America. Bearing the name *Tucino*, 747-357 Combi HB-IGG was photographed at Geneva set against a typically Swiss backdrop of snow-covered hills

Left Apart from two Series 200 aircraft, the whole KLM 'Jumbo' fleet is comprised of Stretched Upper Deck variants, over half of which are -400s. Three -300 Combis were delivered in 1983 and, unlike most airlines, the Dutch carrier was obviously very impressed with the new type – so much so that during 1985/86 ten of the -200s were modified and fitted with a Stretched Upper Deck. The first of those aircraft, 747-206B(SUD/SCD) PH-BUH *Dr Albert Plesman* is seen about to make contact with Kai Tak's runway 13

Above One of KLM's 'true' -300s, 747-306 Combi PH-BUV *Sir Geoffrey de Havilland*, rotates from runway 24L at Schiphol. This particular aircraft, which first flew in August 1984, was the 600th 'Jumbo' built, and was previously operated by the airline as N4551N. In this photograph the Side Cargo Door is clearly visible on the port side of the fuselage, aft of the wing

B747-400

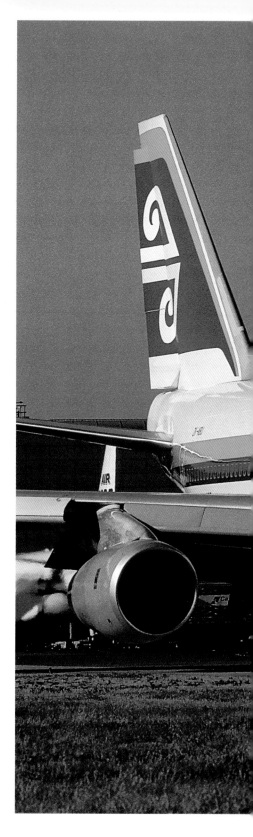

The next variant of the 747, the Series 400, is currently the world's largest, heaviest and most powerful airliner, and is the only variant of the 'Jumbo' now in production. Soon after it was announced in May 1985 orders literally poured in, and deposits had been paid on well over 100 by the time the first airframe was rolled out on 26 January 1988. At first glance the -400 is difficult to distinguish from the -300, which is not overly surprising as both types share a common fuselage. However, there the resemblance ends. The wings are structurally re-designed with aluminium-lithium alloy skin panels, thus saving about 2722 kg (6000 lb) in weight, and they have a span increased by 1.83 m (6 ft).

The most striking visual features, however, are two large 1.83 m (6 ft) high winglets, which improve the aerodynamics of the aircraft. The -400 also has an increased fuel capacity, including fuel tanks inside the horizontal tail which, added to the lighter and redesigned wing, gives a range increase of over 1000 miles on the -300. Indeed Boeing claim fuel savings of 24 per cent compared to the Series 200. The three engine manufacturers which supply powerplants for the 747 have all provided improved versions of their respective products, thus allowing the maximum take-off weight to increase to 394,632 kg (870,000 lb). Of the engine manufacturers, Rolls-Royce power the least number of 747s – however, an increasing number of customers are specifying the RB211 engine for their series -400s.

When the -400 was first announced the Rolls-Royce RB211-524G engine was the most powerful available, producing a thrust of 56,000 lb. Now the RB211-524L is available, and the company ultimately hopes to offer an RB211 with a thrust of 80,000 lb. There is no doubt that the RB211 is currently the most powerful, yet most fuel efficient, engine available today, and for this reason it has just been announced that the Rolls-Royce-

Right The 747-400 is proving to be a very popular aircraft, and by the end of December 1993 a total of 445 had been ordered, of which 200 had been delivered, and it is likely that the type will remain in production till the end of the century. Air New Zealand has three -419s in use, with a fourth on order. The third aircraft, ZK-NBU, was delivered in September 1992

powered 747-400s of Qantas have been authorised to increase their maximum take-off weight to 397,000 kg (875,000 lb). This permits the airline to carry up to 15 extra passengers, or their equivalent weight in cargo, on the ultra long haul 12,050 km (6500 nm) 14-hour, 45-minute journey between Los Angeles and Sydney. The airline will also make use of this allowance on the Singapore–London sector.

The -400 features a new advanced 'glass' cockpit, with analogue displays replaced by multi-colour electronic displays which, according to Boeing,

Above Powered by four Rolls-Royce RB211-524G engines, Air New Zealand's ZK-NBS flares for landing on runway 26L at Gatwick. This was the airline's first 747-400, and it was delivered in December 1989. For some reason it is the only -400 allocated a name, having been christened *Mataatua*. The airline's -419s are in a 16/36/384 passenger configuration, with the upper deck reserved exclusively for business-class passengers, whilst the 16 first-class are seated in the forward section of the nose. In both compartments seating is 2x2, in comparison to the 3x4x3 in economy

Right Air New Zealand uses its 747-419s primarily on routes from Auckland to Frankfurt and London, with a stop-over in Los Angeles – total flight time for the Frankfurt–Auckland flight is an amazing 24 hours and 25 minutes to cover the 19,793 km journey. The airline operates four flights a week from the UK, and they are normally always full. Approaching holding point 'E' at Gatwick is ZK-NBT, the airline's second series -419

reduce cockpit workload by at least a third, and possibly by as much as a half. For this reason the aircraft can be flown with a cockpit crew of only two pilots. With the increased range Boeing have made provision for crew rest areas, with a small space behind the cockpit available for pilots, whilst cabin crews have a rest area fitted with bunks at the rear of the passenger cabin. Due to the range of some sectors these facilities also enable an airline to carry extra crew members to share the workload by working in shifts.

Boeing's sales teams found that the Combi variant proved extremely popular with airlines, so it was logical, therefore, that such a version of the -400 should be made available, as was an SR variant for Japanese customers All Nippon and Japan Air Lines. This latter variant is known as the -400(D), and the two airlines mentioned have a seating configuration of 569 and 568 passengers respectively. This version also dispenses with the winglets – apparently on the short sectors the type is employed on, the fuel saving of an aircraft with winglets is negligible. It is therefore more cost effective to dispense with the winglets, and the associated increase in weight, altogether.

The majority of other -400 operators have a seating capacity in the range of 380-450 passengers. The total of course depends very much on the ratio of first, business and economy class seats. A typical seat pitch in economy for instance would be 34 in, yet in first class this could be as much as 61 in. As an example, compare the seating capacity and ratio of first/business/economy seats of 747-400s operated by KLM and United Airlines. The Dutch carrier seats a total of 387 passengers in an 18/105/264 configuration, whilst United seat 436 in an 18/68/350 configuration, with a greater emphasis on economy and less in business class. I should point out that the KLM configuration applies to the 'standard' -400s, and not the Side Cargo Door Combi variants which the airline also operates.

Maiden flight of the first 747-400, the 696th 'Jumbo' built, took place on 29 April 1988. This aircraft, registered N401PW, was destined for launch customer Northwest Airlines, although it was first put through its paces in order to gain type certification – it also broke yet another record during these flights. On 27 June at Moses Lake airfield in Washington it claimed the world record for the heaviest take-off at 404,994 kg (892,450 lb), before eventually being handed over to the customer in late 1989 as N661US. The honour of the first 747-400 to be actually delivered to a customer for use was bestowed upon Cathay Pacific's VR-HOO, which was delivered to Hong Kong on 28 August 1988, less than a month after its maiden flight.

Lufthansa and Northwest received their first machines soon afterwards. The 747-400 has proved an extremely popular aircraft, and including outstanding orders, it has already outsold the previous best-selling variant, the -200. This is quite an achievement considering that it has been in

Right The -400 is now the most prolific variant in Qantas's large 'Jumbo' fleet, with the 18th, and final, aircraft being delivered in September 1992. All the airline's 747-438s are named after Australian cities, with *City of Darwin* being allocated to VH-OJH, which was photographed climbing out of Auckland, en route to Sydney, as flight QF44

Below right An airline which in the last couple of years has proved to be one of Boeing's best customers is Malaysia Airlines, with orders for the 737-400 alone totalling an amazing 60 airframes – quite what they plan to do with this number remains to be seen. It has also received six 737-500s and a single -300. To supplement its 747 fleet 13 -400s have been ordered to date, half of which have been delivered. The first entered service in November 1989, registered as 9M-MHL (one of two MAS 747-4H6 Combis), and it is seen here on the runway at Heathrow

service just under five years, during which time almost 300 have been built. Some 38 airlines now operate (or have ordered) this variant. A proud moment for Boeing occurred at Everett on 10 September 1993 with the roll-out of the 1000th 747. In front of 18,000 cheering workers, this latest series -400 emerged from the cavernous hangar as executives of Singapore Airlines, the aircraft's owners, looked on. There is also a dedicated freighter variant, designated the -400F, which entered service in late 1993 with Cargolux.

Boeing is currently examining ways of improving the -400 by offering a retrofit kit of minor aerodynamic changes which result in a 0.5 per cent

Above As the 747-400 has six-foot long winglets, most airlines have chosen to display their logo on the outside of this appendage. Cathay Pacific, however, have chosen to repeat their colours on the inside of the winglet, as illustrated in this shot of VR-HOV climbing out of Amsterdam's Schiphol airport

Right The 747-400 has proven very popular with Asian carriers in particular, where there are twice as many operators as in any other continent. Hong Kong-based Cathay Pacific chose the type to supplement its large fleet of -200s and -300s, and the airline has 20 -400s on order as well, two of which are freighters. Photographed on the taxiway at Gatwick is 747-467 VR-HOW. Since this photograph was taken, Cathay has moved its passenger flights from Gatwick to add to the congestion at Heathrow, although the airline's freight services still route via their former UK base

reduction in drag. Although this may not seem like much, over many years of service it could result in a significant amount of money saved in fuel bills per aircraft. The company is also investigating ways of stretching the fuselage of the -400 by some 7 m (23 ft), which would provide seating for a further 70 passengers in a typical three-class layout.

The -400 has so far proven to be an extremely reliable and safe aircraft, although two accidents occurred during 1993. The first of these took place on 12 September at Papeete and involved an Air France machine – the airline has already lost a Series-100 and a -200 in accidents. The aircraft concerned was F-GITA which, after landing in good weather on this tropical paradise, inexplicably veered off the runway and came to rest on the beach, with the nose section immersed in shallow water. Fortunately there were no injuries amongst the 272 passengers and crew, and it is likely that the aircraft will be repaired.

The second accident happened on 4 November, and again the aircraft ended up in the water. On this occasion the victim was China Airlines aircraft B-165, which was only a few months old. Whilst landing on runway 13 at Hong Kong's Kai Tak airport in heavy rain and strong winds, caused by a nearby typhoon, it quickly became apparent to the crew that the aircraft was unlikely to be stopped in the length of the runway. The pilot then apparently tried to turn 90° onto the taxyway at the end of the runway, but the jet was travelling too fast and gently slid backwards into the murky waters of Victoria Harbour. As a tribute to Boeing it floated just like an ocean liner, and all 296 passengers and crew escaped to safety. Afterwards, the 747 remained afloat, but its tail fin was an obstruction to any other movements at the now-closed airport, and it therefore had to be blown off by explosives so that Kai Tak could re-open once again. The 747 has now been recovered from the harbour, but due to the damage caused by the explosion, and the corrosion caused by its immersion in salt water, it is almost certainly beyond economical repair.

Left China Airlines has been a 747 operator since 1975, and it was no surprise when the airline ordered five Series 400s, the last of which, B-165, was delivered on 8 June 1993. This aircraft was to give its owner's barely five month's service before it was lost off the end of the runway at Kai Tak on 4 November 1993, fortunately without any loss of life. Photographed on its take-off roll at Schiphol is sister-ship 747-409 B-163. Note the new control tower at the airport, which is currently the highest in Europe

Above left Eva Air, a member of the Evergreen Group, is a new Taiwanese airline which was formed in 1989. The airline has a fleet of new Boeing 767-300ERs and 747-400s to compete with China Airlines on international routes, and also has MD-11s on order. Its first service to Europe was a Taipei–Bangkok–Vienna route, which has since been extended to London/Gatwick as well. Initially, scheduled services were performed by the 767s until sufficient numbers of 747s had been delivered. Photographed on the inaugural Eva Air 747-400 flight into Gatwick on 29 June 1993 is 747-45E B-16401. The airline received its eighth, and final, -400 in December 1994, four of which are Combis

Left Once purely a domestic carrier, All Nippon Airways now competes on the international stage with Japan Air Lines. Boeing 747-400s are gradually replacing their earlier -200s used on the Tokyo–Heathrow route. This fast-growing airline has 26 -400s on order, some 16 of which have been delivered. Of these, nine will be the -400(D) model for high density/short-haul domestic routes, which are configured for 27 business-class and 542 economy-class seats. The airline's very first 747-481, JA8094, is illustrated at Heathrow in June 1993

Above All Nippon's eighth 747-481(D) JA8963 was delivered on 31 August 1993, although its colour scheme differed somewhat from the other -400s currently in the ANA fleet. To celebrate the airline's 500-millionth passenger, they asked school children to send in their ideas for a special one-off celebratory scheme. The winning entry was designed by a 12-year-old girl, with creatures of the sea as its theme, the emphasis being particularly placed on the whale – rather odd really for a nation which, despite international outcry, still slaughters 300 of the creatures a year for 'scientific purposes'. This special livery has proven to be a hugely successful PR exercise, and ANA has had thousands of calls from people wanting to book flights on 'The Whale'. This is generating an enormous amount of increased revenue, and may be the reason why ANA has decided to adopt the scheme for one of its 767s as well *(All Nippon Airways)*

Above This general shot of the pre-delivery and flight test ramp at Everett shows a single 767 and seven 747-400s from, left to right, Japan Air Lines (two), Air China, Japan Air Lines again, Air France, British Airways and Korean Air, while in the foreground is a Boeing 767 destined for Malev

Above right During the summer of 1991 Air Canada acquired three 747-433 Combis for use on European services, supplementing the same number of Series 100s and -200s. Photographed on approach to Heathrow is 747-433 Combi C-GAGL. Note the cheatline colours are repeated on the outside of the winglets

Right Before a new 747 receives its many coats of paint, and customer livery, it has to be subjected to the lengthy and time consuming process of masking off areas not be painted. In this photograph, taken inside the Everett paint shop, the upper and lower fuselages have been masked off to allow the red cheatline to be sprayed on to this Air Canada 747-433 *(Boeing Airplane Company)*

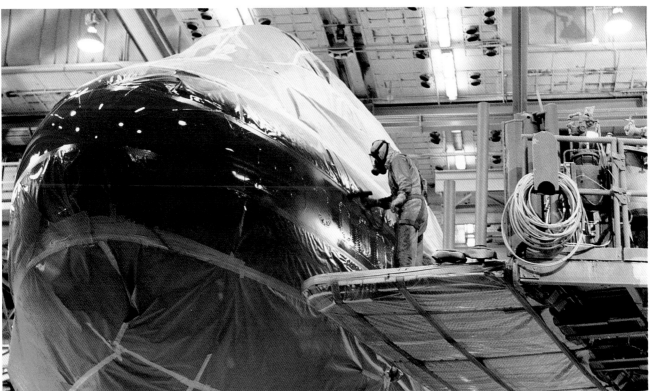

Above left Unlike the Series 100, sales of the -400 in the US have proven to be very disappointing, with only two airlines operating the type – the same number of airlines operate the aircraft north of the 49th parallel in Canada which, although larger geographically, has only a fraction of the population. United Airlines flies an increasing number of -400s, including two of which have just been purchased after being stored in the desert for some while, unwanted by Northwest who initially ordered them. It will take a few months to ready these aircraft for service, after which they will join 24 already in use – incredibly, a further 21 are on order. Photographed at Auckland is 747-422 N178UA

Left Alongside its fleet of elderly Series 100s, and the -200s of 1980s vintage, Northwest operates ten -400s, the first of which was delivered in December 1989. These aircraft are used predominantly on transpacific routes, particularly to Tokyo, leaving the ageing -100s to support DC-10s on European routes. Seen on push-back from its gate at Detroit Metropolitan airport is 747-451 N667US

Above The Dutch carrier KLM has recently taken delivery of its 16th, and final, 747-406, most of which are Combis, whilst two -406F freighters are on order for 1996 delivery. These aircraft supplement the fleet of -200 and -300 aircraft on the airline's intercontinental routes, supported by MD-11s, which are currently being delivered to replace the DC-10s. Although the earlier 'Jumbos' are named after rivers and famous people, the -400s are named after cities served by the type, the initial letter often corresponding to the last letter of the aircraft's registration. For example, 747-406 Combi PH-BFF is named *City of Freetown*, and was photographed a fraction of a second away from touchdown on runway 06R at Schiphol

Above South African Airways received its fourth 747-444 on 5 October 1993, and the type has now replaced earlier variants on services to London/Heathrow. Photographed in weather conditions which, for a change, resemble Johannesburg rather than London, ZS-SAX *Kempton Park* is about to line-up on Heathrow's runway 09R

Left Air France has taken delivery of 12 Series 400s, five of which are Combis, whilst the acquisition of UTA has seen a further two join the fleet. The carrier was destined to be the first recipient of the -400 freighter, five of which are on order, though these plans have slipped and the first two -400Fs were delivered to Cargolux at the end of 1993 instead. Note that the leading-edge slats are still deployed in this shot of 747-428 Combi F-GISE climbing out of Sydney's Kingsford-Smith International airport

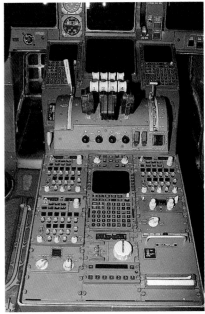

Above This view of the centre console of the 747-400 shows much of the communications equipment, as well as throttles, speed brakes, flaps and trim adjusters

Left The modern cockpit of the Series 400 features few analogue instruments – instead, much of the information required is held on a computer menu, and can be called up for display on the Electronic Flight Information System (EFIS) screens as and when required

Above Some say that the initials BA stand for 'Boeing Always', and there is no doubt that British Airways is one of Boeing's best customers, with large fleets of all the types currently in production, as well as orders for the 777, which is due to fly this year. Despite the acquisition of large numbers of 747-400s, the airline seems to be in no hurry to dispose of its older variants. So far 28 747-436s have been delivered, one of which is leased/operated by subsidiary British Asia, with deposits for a further 22 currently in place – once these orders have been completed, British Airways will boast world's largest fleet of 747-400s. These machines are named after British cities, including *City of Lincoln*, which is allocated to G-BNLT

Above right Singapore Airlines operates an ever increasing fleet of 'Jumbos', second only to Japan Air Lines. The Japanese carrier also currently has the world's largest 747-400 fleet in service, with 30 aircraft on strength, just ahead of British Airways. The Singaporean carrier has 22 -400s on strength, with a further 21 on order. This will put it ahead of JAL, and close to challenging BA for the number one position in regards to -400s in service – an incredible achievement for the small island nation. Photographed here about to land at Brussels National airport is 747-412 9V-SMM. As mentioned in an earlier chapter, Singapore Airlines have dubbed their 747-300s 'BIG TOP', and the -400s duly had to go one better and are known as 'MEGATOP'! Note the small hump midway along the spine – this is for satellite communications equipment

Right A shot of just a small part of the massive 747 assembly hangar at Everett showing four -400s in advanced stages of production *(Boeing Airplane Company)*

Specification and Users

B747-100	
First flight date	9 February 1969
Max accommodation	516
Wing span	59.64 m (195 ft 8 in)
Length	70.66 m (231 ft 10 in)
Height	19.33 m (63 ft 5 in)
Max take-off weight	340,195 kg (750,000 lb)
Max cruising speed	973 km/h (604 mph)
Max range	8895 km (5527miles)
Service ceiling	13,715 m (45,000 ft)

B747-200	
First flight date	11 October 1970
Max accommodation	516
Wing span	59.64 m (195 ft 8 in)
Length	70.66 m (231 ft 10 in)
Height	19.33 m (63 ft 5 in)
Max take-off weight	377,840 kg (833,000 lb)
Max cruising speed	981 km/h (610 mph)
Max range	13,158 km (8176 miles)
Service ceiling	13,715 m (45,000 ft)

B747-300	
First flight date	5 October 1982
Max accommodation	563
Wing span	59.64 m (195 ft 8 in)
Length	70.66 m (231 ft 10 in)
Height	19.33 m (63 ft 5 in)
Max take-off weight	377,840 kg (833,000 lb)
Max cruising speed	996 km/h (619 mph)
Max range	10,463 km (6502 miles)
Service ceiling	13,715 m (45,000 ft)

B747-400	
First flight date	29 April 1988
Max accommodation	569
Wing span	64.31 m (211 ft 0 in)
Length	70.66 m (231 ft 10 in)
Height	19.33 m (63 ft 5 in)
Max take-off weight	397,000 kg (875,000 lb)
Max cruising speed	985 km/h (612 mph)
Max range	15,410 km (8320 miles)
Service ceiling	13,715 m (45,000 ft)

B747SP	
First flight date	4 July 1975
Max accommodation	440
Wing span	59.64 m (195 ft 8 in)
Length	56.31 m (184 ft 9 in)
Height	19.94 m (65 ft 5 in)
Max take-off weight	299,376 kg (660,000 lb)
Max cruising speed	996 km/h (619 mph)
Max range	16,450 km (10,222 miles)
Service ceiling	13,715 m (45,000 ft)

Operators of the 747

By the end of December 1993 a total of 1179 747s had been ordered, over 1000 of which had been delivered. Of this total, 465 are Series 400s, and this number is likely to rise by several hundred more before production finally ends. The list below contains the names of those operators who currently fly the 747, as well as those who no longer do so, or indeed no longer exist, as well as those who have the type on order.

Aer Lingus, Aerolineas Argentinas, Air Afrique, Air Algerie, Air Canada, Air Europe, Air France, Air Gabon, Air Hong Kong, Air India, Air Jamaica, Air Lanka, Air Madagascar, Air Mauritius, Air Namibia, Air National, Air New Zealand, Air Pacific, Air Portugal, Air Siam, Air Zaire, Alia/Royal Jordanian, Alitalia, All Nippon, America West, American Airlines, Asiana, Atlas Air, Avianca, BOAC/British Airways, Braniff, British Airtours, British Asia Airways, British Caledonian, Brunei Government, CAAC/Air China, Cameroon Airlines, Cargolux, Cathay Pacific, China Airlines, Condor, Continental, Corsair, CP Air/Canadian Airlines International, Delta, Dominicana, Eastern Airlines, Egyptair, El Al, Eva Air, Evergreen, Federal Express, Flying Tigers, Garuda Indonesia, German Cargo, Gulf Air, Hawaii Express, Highland Express, Iberia, Icelandair, Iraqi Airways, Iran Air, Imperial Iranian Air Force, Japan Air Lines, Japan Asia, Japanese Government, Japan Universal System Transport, Jet 24, Kalitta American, Kenya Airways, KLM, Korean Air, Kuwait Airways, Lionair, Lufthansa, Malaysian Airlines, Mandarin Airlines, Martinair, Metro International, Middle East Airlines, NASA, Nationair, National Airlines, Nigeria Airways, Nippon Cargo Airlines, Northwest (Orient), Olympic, Oman Government, Overseas National, Pakistan International, Pan American, People Express, Philippine Airlines, Polar Air Cargo, Qantas, Royal Air Maroc, Sabena, Saha Air, SAS, Saudia, Saudi Government, Scanair, Seaboard World, Singapore, South African Airlines, Southern Air Transport, Swan Airlines, Swissair, Syrianair, Tajik Air, Thai International, Tower Air, Trans International/Transamerica, Trans Mediterranean, Trans World Airlines, United Airlines, United Arab Emirates Government, United Parcel Service, USAF, UTA, Varig, Viasa, Virgin Atlantic, Wardair, World Airways